First published in Great Britain in 2023 by

Bristol University Press
University of Bristol
1–9 Old Park Hill
Bristol
BS2 8BB
UK
t: +44 (0)117 374 6645
e: bup-info@bristol.ac.uk

Details of international sales and distribution partners are available at
bristoluniversitypress.co.uk

© Bristol University Press 2023

British Library Cataloguing in Publication Data
A catalogue record for this book is available from the British Library

ISBN 978-1-5292-2849-6 hardcover
ISBN 978-1-5292-2851-9 ePdf
ISBN 978-1-5292-2850-2 ePub

The right of Yvon Dandurand and Jon Heidt to be identified as authors of this
work has been asserted by them in accordance with the Copyright, Designs
and Patents Act 1988.

Cover design: Bristol University Press
Front cover image: iStock/smartboy10

Bristol University Press uses environmentally responsible
print partners.

Printed in Great Britain by CPI Group (UK) Ltd,
Croydon, CR0 4YY

FSC
www.fsc.org
MIX
Paper from
responsible sources
FSC® C013604

D1477744

YVON DANDURAND AND JON HEIDT

YOUTH CRIME PREVENTION AND SPORTS

An Evaluation of Sport-Based Programmes
and Their Effectiveness

BRISTOL
UNIVERSITY
PRESS

Contents

List of Figures

List of Abbreviations

CDP	coach development programme
FIFA	International Federation of Association Football
MMA	mixed martial arts
PYD	positive youth development
RFPP	Risk Factor Prevention Paradigm
TFL	transformational leadership
UN	United Nations
UNODC	United Nations Office on Drugs and Crime

About the Authors

Yvon Dandurand is a criminologist, Professor Emeritus at the School of Criminology and Criminal Justice, and Associate Emeritus at the South Asian Studies Institute, University of the Fraser Valley, British Columbia, Canada, as well as Fellow and Senior Associate of the International Centre for Criminal Law Reform and Criminal Justice Policy, a United Nations affiliated research institute. He specializes in comparative criminal justice research and has been extensively involved in criminal justice reform, crime prevention, and policy development projects. A lot of his research is concerned with delineating effective strategies to prevent crime and to counter organized crime.

Jon Heidt holds a PhD in Criminology from Simon Fraser University (2012) and is Associate Professor of Criminology at the University of the Fraser Valley. His work has been in several academic journals including *Critical Criminology* and *The Journal of Theoretical and Philosophical Criminology*. He co-authored, with Johannes Wheeldon, a textbook titled *Introducing Criminological Thinking: Maps, Theories, and Understanding* (Sage, 2015). He has recently completed a book on cannabis legalization titled *Cannabis Criminology: From Moral Panics to Responsive Regulation* (Routledge, forthcoming).

Acknowledgements

The authors gratefully acknowledge the support they received from the International Centre for Criminal Law Reform and Criminal Justice Policy, the Thailand Institute of Justice, and especially the South Asian Studies Institute, University of the Fraser Valley, and its director, Dr Satwinder Bains.

A key part of the review presented in this book was made possible by the financial support of the Crime Reduction Research Programme, British Columbia Ministry of Public Safety and Solicitor General.

Our thanks to our student researchers, Tyler Falk, Christopher Wiebe, and Landon Kaetler, and our thanks also to Rebecca Tomlinson and Freya Trand of Bristol University Press, and Sophia Unger for their valuable editorial assistance.

Introduction

Sport-based crime prevention enjoys a level of popularity and political support which, despite the boastful claims of its supporters, is not totally justified by its meagre success. Many sport-based youth programmes purport to prevent youth crime or youth involvement in gangs. Indeed, sports stand with several other activities (for example, education, mentoring, religious teaching, and volunteering) that may spur positive social development among children and youth.

Crime prevention strategies have tried to build on the popularity and benefits of sports activities to promote youth development and to influence risk and resiliency factors associated with criminal involvement. Various sport-based crime prevention programmes, usually targeting youth crime, have been implemented over the last two decades. Unfortunately, they are rarely subjected to anything close to a rigorous evaluation. As a result, many of these programmes continue to be funded despite their overly ambitious crime prevention objectives, the vague rationales for their activities, and the near-total absence of evidence of their impact on youth crime.

As one searches for new ideas to improve youth crime prevention, it is difficult to ignore the growing popularity of sport-based crime prevention programmes. Given the magnitude of social investments in such programmes and the programmes' own unrelenting claims of success, one might reasonably expect to encounter many carefully designed and monitored programmes. Instead, what one finds is better described as the triumph of enthusiasm over reason. Proponents of these programmes are undeterred by their lack of demonstrable crime prevention outcomes.

At best, the idea of preventing crime through sports activities is based on a hazy concept that perpetuates itself without clear definitions, a coherent theoretical basis, or any persuasive empirical evidence. Unfortunately, that kind of unbridled enthusiasm for intuitively attractive but poorly informed or uncritical interventions is not uncommon in the field of crime prevention. Also disconcerting is the fact that unsuccessful or unproven prevention programmes are rarely abandoned or discarded; their champions are not that easily persuaded to change their strategies. The field of crime prevention often resembles a desert of 'walking dead' concepts where zombie ideas never die.

Strangely, criminology has not paid significant attention to the role of sports in crime prevention. Other than a passing reference to sport-based crime prevention programmes and their promises in textbooks on crime prevention (Waller, 2014; Elliott and Fagan, 2017) or a brief acknowledgment in 'sport criminology' (Groombridge, 2017), most of the relevant research has emerged in other disciplines.

The relationship between sport and crime is difficult to disentangle. There is controversy around whether sport participation should be regarded as a protective or risk factor in relation to youth crime. Research on the relationship between sport participation and subsequent illegal behaviour failed to establish clearly whether sport participation acts as a preventive measure or an additional risk factor for illegal behaviour during youth or later in life. If sport participation acted as a sufficient deterrent of future crime activities, one would expect not to find serious criminals among graduates of elite business or law schools, particularly those who had every opportunity to participate in sports and did. That this is not so is painfully obvious as one considers the frequency with which these socially advantaged professionals are involved in various frauds, commercial and financial crimes, money laundering, tax evasion, and the like. Moreover, some studies have revealed a troubling link between sport participation and youth involvement in certain types of delinquency, including violence and problematic alcohol use (Stansfield, 2017). Others have noted the links between acquired brain injury, through sports and other risk-taking activities, and youth crime (Williams, 2012).

It is very clear that involvement in sport can impact different aspects of one's personality and social setting in both positive and negative ways. It is also clear that risk-based theories of youth crime prevention rest on shaky evidence and that positive youth development (PYD) interventions, through sports or other forms of intervention, still have to demonstrate how they can produce tangible crime prevention outcomes.

There remains a critical need for further research and theory to identify the contexts and processes through which sport participation may contribute to crime prevention. In particular, further research is needed on how and under what circumstances sports contribute to youth development and the extent to which helping youth to develop human, social, and psychological capital prevents criminal behaviour or encourages desistance from crime.

This book is based in part on a review of existing sport-based crime prevention programmes in British Columbia (Canada) and interviews with coaches and programme facilitators. It also draws on existing research on evidence-based practices in the field of sport and crime prevention and their theoretical foundations. Finally, the book benefited from the hard discussions held during a three-day international expert group meeting organized around the same subject by the Thailand Institute of Justice and the United Nations Office on Drugs and Crime (UNODC), in Bangkok, in December 2019 (United Nations, 2020).

The book takes stock of research evidence on the impact of sport-based crime prevention programmes on youth crime and gang recruitment. It also attempts to conceptualize the links between criminological theory, youth development, and sport-based crime prevention programmes. One of its aims is to identify emerging successful practices for promoting youth development through sport-based programmes for crime prevention purposes. The goal is to maximize the value and potential impact of crime prevention interventions through sports until rigorous programme evaluations can provide more specific programme development guidance.

The book starts with a discussion of crime prevention through sports, including some working definitions, and Chapters 2, 3, and 4, respectively, examine the role of sport participation and sport-based programmes at each of three levels of crime prevention intervention. There is a long-standing tradition in the crime prevention field of distinguishing between these three complementary levels of intervention. The primary level involves interventions that address social, environmental, or situational conditions associated with various criminal activities. The secondary level includes interventions that target individuals or groups known or assumed to be at risk of criminal involvement. The tertiary level entails a range of interventions within or outside the criminal justice system to prevent individuals already engaged in criminal activity from reoffending and encouraging them to desist from crime while successfully reintegrating into society. It is often assumed that sports activities have the potential to contribute to crime prevention at all three levels but, as yet, the evidence to support this assumption is still sparse.

This categorization of levels of crime prevention interventions can help to distinguish between different approaches to sport-based interventions. At the primary level, one finds sport-based programmes that generally promote sport participation in school, after school, or in the community to promote individual development, community development, or more generally, social development. At the secondary level, one finds programmes that purportedly target at-risk individuals or groups and tend to use sport as a platform for delivering other interventions. These interventions can be either strength- or deficit-based, depending on the extent that they focus on mitigating risk factors or enhancing resiliency factors. At the tertiary level, the interventions are part of rehabilitation, re-education, or reintegration programmes to promote desistance from crime and prevent reoffending.

Chapter 5 presents an attempt to conceptualize the links between criminological theory and sport-based crime prevention programmes. It includes an effort to clarify existing concepts and connect them to the theories commonly used to understand youth crime and desistance from crime. The chapter attempts to articulate a theory of change, a prerequisite to forming a cogent programme logic model and conducting programme evaluations.

Since sport-based crime prevention initiatives will be around for a long time, no matter how much or how little evidence may be uncovered about their impact, the more theoretical chapter is followed by Chapter 6, which identifies good practices within these programmes. It addresses the question of what, if anything, communities and crime prevention proponents can do to maximize their investments in sport-based programmes from the points of view of peace, public safety, and crime prevention.

Chapter 7 focuses on the role of coaches and the impact of coaching practices on youth development, not only because existing research emphasizes the crucial importance of that role, but also because of the considerable amount of interest expressed in how they could improve their own practices by the coaches and programme facilitators who were contacted during the review.

Chapter 8 concludes the book with a discussion of the evaluation of sport-based crime prevention programmes and a reflection on their evaluability.

ONE

Youth Crime Prevention: Myths and Reality

At the beginning of a book purporting to review the impact of sport-based crime prevention initiatives, one might expect a clear definition of 'sport-based crime prevention'. The problem with this, unfortunately, is that proponents of that approach tend to leave it vague, and thus avoid scrutiny with respect to its actual impact. Under the cover of haziness, various sport-based crime prevention initiatives can avoid articulating their own logic or explaining how exactly, or on the basis of what evidence, the sports activities they support can logically be associated with crime prevention. The fact is that, as will be discussed in the next chapter, there is little evidence that participation in sport prevents crime or encourages desistance from crime. That observation alone should be enough to disqualify many sports programmes from being subsidized through crime prevention budgets. However, it certainly does not dissuade many from making unsubstantiated claims about the crime prevention impact of sport-based programmes. When they run short of evidence or arguments, proponents of these initiatives are quick to suggest that even if crime prevention is not their main goal, it is nevertheless one of the programmes' by-products.

The concept of sport-based crime prevention is still in need of standard definitions, including operational definitions of what constitutes a sport-based intervention or programme other than the inclusion of a sport-related component. There is no terminology to differentiate between programmes where sport is the sole activity, those that combine sport with other social interventions (for example, using sport as a 'hook' to recruit youth), and those where sport is a marginal aspect of the programme. The centrality of sport in such programmes can vary considerably. In many instances, sport is only one of several activities in which participants take part and it is therefore very difficult to identify or quantify sport-specific effects. In some crime prevention programmes, sport participation does not even play a role; it is considered sufficient in some programmes to expose youth to successful athletes or sports personalities as role models or motivational speakers.

Sport is itself not always defined clearly within crime prevention initiatives. Sometimes it refers to physical exercise on its own. A distinction is not always explicitly made between competitive sports that could potentially involve violent physical contact, and other sport activities where one is mostly competing against oneself.

Sport participation is also in need of a clearer definition, as participation in sport can take many forms, whether it is as a player or athlete, a coach or leader, a referee or volunteer, or even as a spectator. All these forms of participation have been suggested as means to prevent youth crime. The notion of participation is used in an inconsistent manner, covering any form or level of participation in just about any capacity, including recruiting youth to coach or facilitate sports activities for younger age groups, or even mere participation as a spectator. The latter has been associated with its own problems (problem alcohol use, violent confrontations, hooliganism, riots, even communal violence) and limited positive impact (Groombridge, 2017; Copus and Laqueur, 2019). In fact, there is much controversy around whether sport participation should be regarded as a protective or a risk factor for the development of juvenile delinquency.

Research on the relationship between sport participation and subsequent illegal behaviour does not clearly establish whether sport participation acts as a preventative measure or a risk factor for illegal behaviour later in life (Davis and Menard, 2013). Participation in sport activities does not automatically enhance prosocial behaviour (Scheithauer, Leppin, and Hess, 2020). A study of the short-term and long-term impacts of school-based youth sport participation on adult illegal behaviour, by Davis and Menard (2013), suggests that, in general, sport participation has very little, if any, direct impact on illegal behaviour. Moreover, theoretical and empirical knowledge about the relationship between sport participation and juvenile delinquency are both lacking (Spruit et al, 2016).

What is also missing, as will be further discussed in Chapter 5, is a clear and coherent theoretical conception of sport-based crime prevention programmes, or a theory of change that can explain how and why such programmes work and how they should be implemented (Hartman, 2003).

The claims of sport-based programmes

Since antiquity, sports have been seen as a vehicle for moral education and physical and mental health. Today, there is a growing interest in trying to define the place that sports and sport-based interventions can occupy in implementing social policies, from social development (Skinner and Zakus, 2008; Coalter, 2010a, 2010b, 2012, 2013; Hartmann and Kwauk, 2011; Dudfield and Dingwall-Smith, 2015; United Nations, 2017), conflict prevention, the promotion of social cohesion or peacebuilding (Giulianotti, 2004, 2011), to crime prevention (United Nations Office on Drugs and Crime, 2017, 2020a), the prevention of violent extremism (Johns, Grossman, and McDonald, 2014; Samuel, 2018; United Nations Office on Drugs and Crime, 2020b), or the social reintegration of offenders (Draper et al, 2013; Meek, 2014).

The international interest in sport and development is often connected with other efforts to use sport for the purposes of social intervention (Coalter, 2010, 2013; Hartmann and Kwauk,

2011). Various sport-based crime prevention programmes, usually targeting youth crime, have been implemented almost everywhere over the last two decades. Internationally, the United Nations General Assembly, in its Resolution 74/170 titled 'Integrating sport into youth crime prevention and criminal justice strategies', encouraged Member States to use sport-based activities more widely to promote primary, secondary, and tertiary prevention of youth crime and the social reintegration of young offenders. In September 2020, the International Federation of Association Football (FIFA) announced that it was partnering with the UNODC to fight corruption in sports – something one might consider long overdue – sweetened by a promise to 'consider ways in which football can be used as a vehicle to strengthen youth resilience to crime and substance use through the provision of life skills training' (FIFA, 2020). The partnership also promised to facilitate social inclusion through football in the context of youth crime prevention. Moreover, sport-based interventions, often targeting youth in search of a sense of belonging or an identity, are also promoted as a means to prevent violent extremism (RAN Centre of Excellence, 2019; United Nations Office on Drugs and Crime, 2020b) and are proposed as crucial tools, together with educational and vocational activities, in the rehabilitation of radicalized individuals (Richardson, Cameron, and Berlouis, 2017).

However, while the international community marketed sport as an effective development tool, much less effort went into conceptualizing, organizing and structuring the whole sport and development field (Coalter, 2006). For Hartmann and Kwauk (2011: 285–6), '(w)ith little more than anecdotal evidence, beliefs about the impact of sport in development are driven mainly by heartfelt narratives, evocative images, and quotable sound bites of individual and community transformation, packaged and delivered more often than not by those running the programs'.

There is no disputing the benefits of physical activity and sports. '*Mens sana in corpore sano*' – a sound mind in a sound body – is still a powerful motto. Billions of dollars are spent each year on physical wellness products and services, much of that sum on exercise equipment, gym memberships, personal trainers, and even virtual coaches. The virtue of personal exercise for wellness and for physical and mental health no longer needs to be sold. There is also evidence that early sport participation may help protect youth against the development of depression, anxiety, and other internalizing behaviours (Sheppard and Mahoney, 2012) and generally predicts better mental health (Doré et al, 2019). Sport and exercise have a positive impact on the physical and mental health of prisoners (Meek, 2014). The benefits of sport and exercise after severe traumatic brain injury have also been documented, including as a means to assist with social reintegration (Quilico et al, 2021).

Sports may be generally good for child and youth development, but so is mothers' milk, good nutrition, good friends, and so many other things. School-based milk distribution programmes, for example, were sometimes sold as a crime prevention initiative. The logic behind this went as follows: students who are hungry cannot fully concentrate on studying or participate in class activities, milk is an efficient way of supplementing the children's nutrition while they are at school, milk improves students' attention which leads to student success, which leads to school retention, which leads to less absenteeism and school dropout, and therefore prevents crime because it is apparently well known that early school abandonment is associated with delinquent behaviour. The question that concerns us here is not whether sport participation can be beneficial to youth, but whether it can produce any direct and lasting effects on youth behaviour, their conformity with social norms, or their desistance from crime.

Before moving to that question, however, it is useful to consider the fact that youth sport participation can also have a negative impact on behaviour. Research does not support the claim that youth sport necessarily fosters positive outcomes. Positive physical and developmental outcomes can accrue from regular participation in sport, but sport participation can also lead to various negative outcomes. Sport experiences vary in terms of the teaching, coaching, and supervision the individuals receive, and so do their effects (Bailey, 2005). High school sport participation, for example, exposes student-athletes to a variety of experiences that can positively and negatively influence their personal development, with coaches playing a particularly influential role in this developmental process (Turgeon et al, 2019).

Negative aspects of sport participation

In some instances, participation in organized sports activities during adolescence may be associated with poor health-related outcomes (for example, injuries, concussions, harmful weight control practices, increased anxiety, stress and burnout, alcohol and drug use) (Bean et al, 2014; Cowan and Taylor, 2016). Promoters of sport-based crime prevention tend to dismiss the negative aspects of sport participation or present them as the results of rare accidental events. Yet traumatic brain injury resulting from sports is a major source of disability among youth and can hardly be discarded as a rarity. Traumatic brain injury is the leading form of acquired brain injury, particularly among young people, resulting mostly from sporting injuries, falls, fights and road accidents (Williams, 2012; Veliz et al, 2019; Veliz, Ryan, and Eckner, 2021). Further, a link has been observed between some forms of criminal behaviour and acquired brain injuries, possibly because risk-taking individuals may be at particular risk of impulsive criminal behaviours, and similarly, at greater risk of engaging in thrill-seeking behaviours where injury is more likely (Williams, 2012).

Contrary to the assumption that sport serves as a protective factor against alcohol and drug use, high school sport participation has also been associated with substance abuse among young adults (Eitle, Turner, and Eitle, 2003). Adolescents' participation in some organized competitive sport was found in some studies to be associated with higher levels of alcohol use (Terry-McElrath, O'Malley, and Johnston, 2011; Farb and Matjasko, 2012) and an increased growth in alcohol use over time (Mays et al, 2010), and early adolescent alcohol use is itself associated with violence, injuries, drunk driving and later alcohol misuse (Hallinberg et al, 2015). It appears that the relationship between sport participation and problem alcohol use depends on participation in sports in combination with other activities (Mays et al, 2010). However, findings are not consistent and the relationship between sports and alcohol use seems to vary according to the type of sport (Hallinberg et al, 2015). With regards to youth mental health, increased alcohol consumption has been linked to sport participation (particularly in certain team sports), and decreases in well-being have been linked to high levels of training, which likely lead to burnout and dropout (Bean et al, 2014).

Social activities around certain sport events are often violent and fuelled by the excessive consumption of alcohol, involving both the youth and their parents or supporters (Rich, Bean, and Apramian, 2014). Violent actions which would be deemed criminal in other contexts may be normalized in certain sport contexts (Engelberg and Moston, 2020). Violence and incivility of players in professional sports has attracted a lot of research attention (Engelberg and Moston, 2020; Ruppé et al, 2020; Sheppard-Marks, Shipway, and Brown, 2020) and its influence on the amateur youth sport culture cannot be easily dismissed.

Some sports activities may ritualize and even legitimize violence and confrontation in connection with certain ideals of masculinity. It is often suggested that sports may lead to the acquisition of aggressive skills and behaviours that could be brought into play outside sport settings. There is evidence that sport-based activities can have a negative impact on youth violence, although both positive and negative impacts are mediated by circumstantial factors (Kreager, 2007; McMahon and Belur, 2013; Stansfield, 2017). Stansfield (2017) argued that the association between sports and delinquency is more nuanced and that the type of sports involvement matters, with some sports having a greater association with delinquency for males than other sports. Moreover, an emphasis on violence in sport may be linked to sexual violence among athletes. The United Nations' expert group emphasized the importance of ensuring that sport-based programmes do not encourage toxic masculinity, confrontations, violence or gender-based violence (United Nations, 2020).

There are other potential negative developmental experiences associated with sport participation that are not always acknowledged by sport-based programmes (stress; social exclusion; discrimination; aggression; physical, sexual, and emotional abuse; and various forms of intimidation and control by coaches and peers). A few studies have revealed, for example, how the aggressive subcultures of some sports have infiltrated high school sport and created negative sport experiences for participants (Fraser-Thomas and Côté, 2009; Gould, Flett and Lauer, 2012; Kendellen and Camiré, 2015). Participation in team sports may encourage minor forms of group offending (for example, cannabis use, underage alcohol use, vandalism) (Davis and Menard, 2013). Coakley (2011) suggested that, unless mentors and coaches instil a philosophy of non-violence and encourage self-control, self-confidence, responsibility, and respect (to both oneself and others), participation in sport may exacerbate or encourage aggression. Stansfield acknowledged that 'the degree to which sports teams or recreational groups support violence and alcohol likely varies highly across type of sport, level of commitment and coaching.' (Stansfield, 2017: 189).

A UK study examined the harmful experiences of children in a sport setting and revealed that disrespectful and emotionally harmful treatment, harmful training, and bullying of young people were commonplace in children's experiences of sport in the UK (Alexander, Stafford, and Lewis, 2011; McMahon and Belur, 2013). In Australia, in a survey designed to explore children's experiences of organized sport, as recounted by young adults between the ages of 18 and 25 years, respondents overwhelmingly identified their sport experience as children as a positive, socially enriching, and fun experience with lasting developmental benefits of participation in organized sport as children, but half of them also reported negative experiences, including emotional and physical harm and sexual harassment (McPherson et al, 2017). The category of abuse most frequently reported by survey respondents was emotional abuse, most often by other children, but also by coaches and other children's parents. Coaches were most frequently named as perpetrators of physical abuse and sexual harassment (Alexander, Stafford, and Lewis, 2011; McPherson et al, 2017).

Most interestingly, a large-scale cross-national study seems to confirm the relationship between youth participation in sport and delinquency, including violence and problematic alcohol use (Stansfield, 2017). The study revealed that higher levels of sports involvement increased involvement in violence, but that the risk of alcohol and drug use behaviour diminished as sport started to occupy a greater part of a youth's time. There seemed to be a turning point where more engagement in sports translated into a reduced risk (Stansfield, 2017).

Several studies have examined the incidence of various forms of child maltreatment in sport (allegations of emotional abuse, bullying and physical abuse, as well as sexual abuse). Children and youth participating in sport, especially girls, are particularly vulnerable to abuse, exploitation, and violence because of their reliance on the support of coaches and others in positions of influence. Sexual, physical, and psychological violence against athletes, from coaches, opponents, and teammates, is still poorly reported or measured (Parent and Fortier, 2017). McPherson and colleagues (2017), summarizing some of the relevant research, also reported that children who have a disability or who have been victims of previous abuse, or who are attracted to members of the same sex, may be more vulnerable to abuse and exclusion in sport may be more vulnerable to an experience of abuse in the context of sport.

Non-accidental violence, abuse, and maltreatment are far more common in sports, particularly competitive sports, than tends to be acknowledged by proponents of sport as a positive development experience for children and youth. There is now irrefutable evidence of considerable presence of child maltreatment in sport, from physical abuse (Alexander, Stafford, and Lewis, 2011; Vertommen et al, 2016), psychological abuse (Vertommen et al, 2016) and bullying (Evans et al, 2016; Nery et al, 2019; Mishna et al, 2019), to sexual abuse (Fasting et al, 2004; Shannon, 2013; Gervis, Rhind and Luzar, 2016; Bjørnseth and Szabo, 2018). Competitive environments, limited supervision, and unstructured time are programme elements perceived as increasing the likelihood of bullying and other aggressive behaviours (Shannon, 2013). Moreover, these negative outcomes may result from underlying social norms, including the acceptance of pain and injury during play and the approval of aggressive behaviour towards opponents in order to win the game (Stafford, Alexander, and Fry et al, 2013).

In addition to research on non-accidental violence in sport and organizational factors that may underpin psychological, physical, or sexual violence in sport (Roberts, Sojo, and Grant, 2020), recent studies have documented the experiences of survivors and victims who experienced gender-based violence in sports and, in particular, being silenced by coaches, members of the sports organizations, and even parents and siblings (Hartmann-Tews, 2021). A range of issues related to child protection and safeguarding in sport, such as emotional abuse, injury, and over-training, are revealed, together with renewed concerns about child, youth, and athlete welfare (Lang and Hartill, 2016). The serious long-term negative physical and psychological consequences of these forms of 'non-accidental violence' for young athletes are well documented (Vertommen et al, 2018; Roberts, Sojo, and Grant, 2020).

That knowledge led to a wealth of safeguarding research aimed at identifying effective and comprehensive approaches for protecting children from harm in sport and addressing individual, interpersonal, cultural, and systemic contributors to child maltreatment in sport (Nite and Nauright, 2020; Roberts, Sojo and Grant, 2020; Hartmann-Tews, 2021; Owusu-Sekyere, Rhind, and Hills, 2021). Safeguarding policies and practices are also beginning to be adopted in various sporting organizations.

At the same time, researchers are beginning to understand that organizational silence and denial of the negative aspects of sport participation **is** a collective-level phenomenon that goes beyond simple wilful blindness towards violence in sports, especially gender-based violence (Hartmann-Tews, 2021). Sport organizations have also demonstrated bystander inaction and a culture of silence on psychological, physical and sexual abuse, despite knowledge or suspicions that coaching personnel or other athletes were acting in harmful ways towards athletes (Parent, 2011, Parent and Fortier, 2017; Roberts, Sojo, and Grant, 2020).

The positive image of sports and the unchallenged cognitive mindset surrounding the presumed individual and social benefits of sports can be linked with an 'organizational culture of affective attachment and identification within sports organizations that leads to value consensus and loyalty more than an open airing of doubts and alternative views' (Hartmann-Tews, 2021: 179). The same unchallenged cognitive mindset has tended to obfuscate the debate around the real impact of sport-based programmes in terms of crime prevention and public safety.

The risk factor prevention paradigm

Youth crime prevention initiatives are typically planned around risk and protective factors based on statistical associations at the group level between those factors and 'problem behaviour'. That approach to the crime prevention enterprise is linked to various attempts to reduce risk factors and, in many ways, serves to justify interventions that single out and target various vulnerable or marginalized youth groups.

Sadly, criminology has played and continues to play a role in 'risk politics', and benefits from the rise of a risk assessment and risk management industry in the public safety sector. That discipline has shown little hesitation to use the simplistic actuarial risk prediction methods that spawned quickly in the fields of crime prevention, offender management, and rehabilitation. That risk management approach, enthusiastically endorsed by policy makers and the public, created what Ropeik (2010) calls a 'risk perception gap', a serious gap between our fears and the facts. Often this has resulted in the further stigmatization of youth and various marginalized groups on the basis of uncritical assumptions and flawed measurement of the risk they represent.

There are several other tendencies in crime prevention that must be resisted: (1) holding on to unjustifiable causal assumptions made on the basis of flimsy actuarial predictions of who is likely to be caught and blamed for crimes instead of who is most likely to commit them; (2) an undiscerning willingness to believe the falsehood that youth crime is committed only by statistically identifiable groups of youth, while all other youths are law abiding; (3) the confusion or confounding of some forms of criminal activity, and a lack of specificity about the kind of crime intended to be prevented; (4) the desire to hold on to the beliefs about the relevance of individual risk factors and the ability of various social interventions to mitigate them; and (5) the cognitive dissonance tolerated between what is known about the overwhelming importance of addressing social and structural causal factors and our collective insistence on controlling individuals. There are others.

There are also several problems with the risk-based approach to crime prevention. For one thing, the approach tends to ignore underlying structural issues and inequalities. Crime is reduced to an individual social adaptation issue and at-risk youth are deemed to be more inclined towards antisocial or criminal behaviour, in part because of their uncaring or incompetent parents. In this 'sport as social control' approach, the focus is on disadvantaged or at-risk youth characterized as a danger or a threat to the community who need to be controlled and socialized through leisure and sporting activity (Chamberlain, 2013). This ideology undergirds countless ineffective interventions which misused investments in crime prevention tend to constantly replicate without any demonstrable results.

The risk factor prevention paradigm (RFPP) rose to prominence during the 1990s and has been the basis for many crime prevention programmes in North America and Western Europe (Armstrong, 2006; Hazel and Bateman, 2021). That paradigm, based on approaches used in medicine and public health, was imported into criminology by Catalano and Hawkins (1996) in their social development model and was central to the Cambridge Study of Delinquent Development (Haines and Case, 2008). Life course developmental theories of offending have been guiding community-based crime prevention programmes, locating them primarily in families, schools, and communities and targeting people before they become involved in crime (Elliott and Fagan, 2017).

At the heart of that paradigm is the simple idea that key factors associated with criminal behaviour can be statistically identified and addressed through prevention methods designed to counteract them and reduce the risk of short-term reoffending. Supported in part by criminal career studies, the paradigm is linked to developmental psychology which suggests that childhood factors can be used to predict behaviour later in life. Since the focus is on individual risk factors such as low intelligence, low empathy, impulsiveness, family problems, abuse, and neglect, the proposed methods of intervention typically consist of 'targeted and intensive work with "problem" children and their families' (Garside, 2009: 42).

While the RFPP has been widely accepted by practitioners and has many elements that are politically attractive, it has been the target of some major criticisms and the evidence of its success has been limited and controversial (Haines and Case, 2008). Numerous theoretical and methodological shortcomings have been identified, including: problems defining and measuring risk; vague and inconsistent use of terms across programmes and studies; the exclusion of social, structural, and political factors in favour of more individualistic ones; and issues with interpreting causality and chains of causation (Farrington, 2000; Armstrong, 2004, 2006;;; Hazel and Bateman, 2021). In addition, the RFPP raises several ethical and practical issues due to the fact that it is often manipulated for short-term political pragmatism (Case and Haines, 2021) and leads to crime prevention policies that often stigmatize groups that are already marginalized (Armstrong, 2006; Case and Haines, 2021; France, Freiberg, and Homel, 2010; Goddard and Myers, 2017. Moreover, '(e)xplaining children's criminality on the basis of risk, treats children as objects whose fate is largely determined by the risks which they embody, rather than regarding them as active individuals with a capacity to make choices (…)' (Hazel and Bateman, 2021: 80).

Properly defining and measuring risk factors has not been as straightforward a process as might have been expected. Factors are not defined consistently or precisely in academic studies (Haines and Case, 2008) and are often not uniform when different programmes are compared to each other; confusion ensues where some risk factors are identified as highly important in one study or programme and then ignored completely in another.

At the most basic level, the RFPP is dominated by reductionist assumptions from developmental psychology which suggest that childhood factors can be used to predict behaviour later in life. The paradigm has also been ruled by an 'empiricist psychometric' approach which assumes that childhood is interpreted as context-free, and development is standardized and linear (France, Freiberg, and Homel, 2010). This has often resulted in the use of narrowly defined and unacceptably vague risk factors. The approach also tends to ignore how young people view risk and how risk is socially constructed (Armstrong, 2004). More importantly perhaps, the paradigm almost completely ignores the fact that risk taking, boundaries testing, occasional challenges to authority, and experimentation with alternate identity and patterns of behaviour, as well as some level of criminal offending, are normal parts of adolescence. According to self-reported offending, it is likely that non-convicted individuals will commit many crimes during their lifetime. For example, in one longitudinal study, more than half of non-convicted males self-reported some form of vandalism or shoplifting, usually during the transition from childhood to adolescence; some form of assault during adolescence/young adulthood; and/or fraud during middle adulthood, although it is likely that they will never be caught (Basto-Pereira and Farrington, 2020: 296–297). The authors concluded: 'Therefore, some types of offending during one's lifetime are expected for the general population, even among non-convicted males' (Basto-Pereira and Farrington, 2020: 297).

Whether these risk factors predict criminal involvement is debatable. Indeed, '(o)ur understanding of the relationship between risk and the behaviour of young people is lacking in many regards' (Paylor, 2010: 31). Perhaps more importantly, the notion of 'risk' itself is more problematic than is usually acknowledged. A typically ignored question, as Farrington (2000: 8) acknowledges, is: 'Risk factors for what?', or exactly what behaviour or potential involvement in criminal activity is being predicted by the actuarial risk measurement methods relied upon.

The focus in many studies and programmes rooted in the RFPP tends to be biological, individual, family, peer, school, neighbourhood, and situational factors. More specifically, the RFPP has been criticized for psycho-reductionism and an overemphasis on immediate, proximate, individualistic factors at the expense of contextual, social, political, structural, and macro-level factors (Haines and Case, 2008). Conversely, political and structural factors such as previous involvement with the criminal justice system, police practice, unemployment, and poverty are not adequately considered (Case and Haines, 2021) when, in reality, many of the risks are connected to social structure, systems of governance, or local barriers (for example, social inclusion) (France, Freiberg, and Homel, 2010). To put it differently, many studies and programmes ignore the fact that involvement with the criminal justice system is itself criminogenic and may contribute to more criminal behaviour and overlook the failures and weaknesses of that system (Goddard and Myers, 2017). Finally, the ethnocentric nature of the RFPP makes its applicability to other areas and cultures problematic, especially considering that many societies are becoming increasingly diverse (Haines and Case, 2008). As Armstrong (2006) remarked, the RFPP has driven policy making down the road of individual adaptation rather than important social reform:

> The risk factor approach also constructs social problems in terms of individual and micro-social risks which occur and are perpetuated within those domains. Thus, poverty, although recognized as a factor associated with high risk, is countered not by economic redistribution but by interventions aimed at supporting individuals at the micro level with the management of their own risk. (Armstrong, 2006)

In addition to omitting key factors from several areas, the RFPP tends to disregard or ignore key processes and mechanisms that contribute to criminal behaviour. In doing so, it often falls into the trap of confusing causation and correlation between variables and misinterpreting causal relationships (France, Freiberg, and Homel, 2010). Farrington (2000), who is arguably the most ardent supporter of this approach, even conceded that there is great difficulty in determining which risk factors are causal and which ones are simply correlated with criminal behaviour. He and others noted that the underlying processes, mechanisms, and developmental pathways must be first established to increase understanding of how and why the behaviour takes place (Farrington, 2000; Basto-Pereira and Farrington, 2020). Goddard (2014) expanded on this criticism and suggested that it is unlikely that risk factor research can provide an insight into the relative importance of different factors because most studies are unable to clearly identify chains of causation.

Haines and Case (2008: 10) concluded 'that risk factor research thus far has functioned as a quantitative, pragmatic, prescriptive and somewhat self-fulfilling exercise'. For them, 'risk factor research and interventions are based on poor science and a flawed evidence base' (Case and Haines, 2010: 20). As a predictive tool, risk factor analysis has limited utility. It might identify an increased probability of committing crime and/or being captured by the criminal justice system among certain population groups with shared characteristics. But at the level of the individuals themselves false positives and false negatives abound. The margin for error is very high. 'This sort of evidence,' Armstrong notes, 'is much more suited to generalizations about groups rather than predictions about individuals' (Armstrong, 2006: 272). Risk factor research has not avoided the ecological inference fallacy, a formal fallacy in the interpretation of statistical data that occurs when inferences about the nature of individuals are deduced from inferences about the group to which those individuals belong. Why is this type of fallacy so easily overlooked within the risk factor prevention paradigm? Is it perhaps because this and other shortcomings of the paradigm are politically and practically attractive? They offer simple and straightforward solutions for difficult problems, while conforming to or confirming some societal biases. The obvious mismatch between the limitations of the research upon which the paradigm rests and the policy and practices it supports is striking (Garside, 2009: 42). Case (2007) explains this appeal in the following passage:

The jewel in the actuarialist crown is the 'risk factor prevention paradigm', a pragmatic crime prevention model that uses risk assessment and survey to identify factors in the key domains of a young person's life (family, school, community, psycho-emotional) that statistically increase the likelihood of (official or self-reported) offending ('risk' factors) or decrease its likelihood ('protective' factors). Identified risk and protective factors are then used to inform 'evidence-led' interventions that aim to reduce risk and prevent offending. This risk-focused crime prevention offers an alternative to more traditional responses to youth offending (treatment, rehabilitation, opportunity reduction) by re-orientating youth justice and crime prevention towards a focus on evidence of risk and protection. (Case, 2007: 92)

The sport-based approach to crime prevention is closely tied to the RFPP. However, once the 'risk factor' paradigm is theoretically and practically problematized and its naïve assumptions about the relationships between 'risk' and youth crime are challenged, the theoretical and logical bases under sport-based crime interventions are revealed to be shaky. Despite increasing clarity that risk prevention does not necessarily lead to successful outcomes, risk prevention remains at the centre of most youth crime prevention initiatives, instead of focusing on ways to support youth development and building youth resilience (Allison et al, 2011). For a growing number of experts and practitioners, 'the key to enhancing the field of youth programming lies in integrating developmental and prevention science and positive youth development' (Allison et al, 2011: 11). As will be discussed in the following chapters, the most promising work in recent years around sport-based crime prevention initiatives came from attempts to conceptually, theoretically, and empirically link positive youth developmental outcomes and risk prevention.

TWO

Sport Participation and Primary Crime Prevention

The sport environment is obviously a popular and important training ground for child and adolescent development. Sports stand with several other activities (for example, education, mentoring, religious teaching, and volunteering) as a potential factor in influencing positive social development among children and youth. Crime prevention strategies have therefore tried to build on the popularity and benefits of sports activities to promote youth development and to influence risk and resiliency factors associated with criminal involvement.

A wide variety of community-based programmes aim to use sport either as a means or as a complementary activity to promote youth development and prevent youth crime. Because of its presumed ability to contribute to moral development (Pennington, 2017), character building and the acquisition of life skills, sport (especially competitive team sport) is frequently promoted as having the potential to contribute to crime prevention or the reduction of antisocial behaviour (Coalter, 2007, 2012). However, these primary-level crime prevention initiatives are seldom explicit about the type of crime they purport to prevent (Groombridge, 2017). Some of them refer generally to deviant or problem behaviour and may include anything from lack of self-discipline, defiance of authority, school absenteeism, or experimentation with drugs, to theft, violent and confrontational behaviour, or contacts with the police. Other initiatives specifically refer to violent behaviour, delinquency, or gang involvement, without specifying the exact behavioural nature of the outcomes to be achieved. There is a great deal of wishful thinking and proselytizing behind many programmes (Giulianotti, 2004).

Despite numerous positive anecdotal accounts, there is still little evidence to support the assumption that sport participation is effective in reducing youth crime (Coakley, 1998). Methodological and practical challenges in evaluating the impact of sport participation explain why there is little definitive/empirical evidence to support the assumption that sport is effective in reducing youth crime. Challenges include identifying what aspects to measure to gauge success, poor-quality data, and difficulties in isolating the impact of sport-based initiatives from other confounding factors. Due to research limitations, it is difficult to reach general conclusions on the effectiveness of these programmes (Public Safety Canada, 2017).

The relationship between sport participation and local crime rates is ambiguous. In fact, any link between sport participation and crime is bound to vary by type of crime, and there are obviously many other variables at play (Brosnan, 2020).

A large-scale survey of 15-year-old German youth appeared to confirm that sports activities do not automatically prevent violence (Mutz and Baur, 2009). A multilevel meta-analysis of 51 published and unpublished studies that examine the relationship between sport participation and juvenile delinquency showed that there is no overall significant association between sport participation and juvenile delinquency, indicating that adolescent athletes are neither more nor less delinquent than non-athletes (Spruit et al, 2016; Spruit et al, 2018a, 2018b). In some of the studies reviewed for the meta-analysis, sample and sports characteristics had a significant but modest moderating effect on the relationship between sport participation and juvenile delinquency. Another systematic analysis of 13 programme evaluations concluded that a modest crime prevention outcome could be observed (Jugl,

Bender, and Lösel, 2021), but only because that analysis used an overbroad and shaky definition of the crime prevention outcome that included various self-reported behaviours and attitude towards crime.

Furthermore, there are clear differences in how young men and young women are impacted by sport involvement. Some programmes have positive outcomes for male participants but increase the likelihood of delinquency for female participants, while others have the opposite effect (Fagan and Lindsey, 2014; Lipowski et al, 2016).

The long-term impact of youth sport participation on illegal behaviour (including adult criminal behaviour) is still not clear. According to Davis and Menard, it is unclear whether sport participation acts as a preventative measure or a risk factor for illegal behaviour (Davis and Menard, 2013). One of the findings of programme evaluations so far is that youth participation in sport, in itself, is unlikely to produce crime prevention outcomes (Caldwell and Smith, 2006; Ehsani, Dehnavi and Heidary, 2012; Davis and Menard, 2013; Groombridge, 2017). In fact, methodologically robust evidence is lacking to support the notion that participation in sports activity can lead to a reduction in antisocial and offending behaviour (Chamberlain, 2013).

Based on available evidence, Hartmann and Kwauk (2011) came to two important conclusions: (1) sport programming and participation do not automatically and inevitably lead to prosocial outcomes and effect; (2) sport programming must be combined with other, non-sport programming and investment in order to achieve broader developmental goals. For these authors, a failure to recognize these points compromises the effectiveness of sport-based initiatives and programming and risks producing the opposite effects of those intended. They add: 'Not to realize these two points is to both overestimate the social power of sport and to underestimate the depth, scale, and scope of the challenges of development, education, and intervention' (Hartmann and Kwauk, 2011: 298).

Depending on their respective goals and design, it is probable that sports programmes are able to divert youth from crime and other problematic activities, contribute to character building or youth development, promote social inclusion, or provide youth with access to prosocial networks and positive role models (Hermens et al, 2017). However, the root causes of youth crime, whether understood at the individual or societal levels, cannot reasonably be expected to be single-handedly addressed by the provision of sport opportunities. Programmes should guard against having overly ambitious objectives (Bailey, 2005). According to the conclusions of an international group of experts convened by the United Nations (2020: 9), 'the power of sports to produce social change should not be overestimated and sport should not be seen as an alternative to public investments in education, access to employment, social services, access to justice, and rehabilitation programmes'.

Character building

An unavoidable question, raised by Coakley (2002) 20 years ago, remains unanswered: 'What leads many people to think that youth sport programmes might solve problems of deviance and violence when research clearly shows that these problems are related to a long history of economic decline, high rates of poverty, and feelings of despair in inner cities?' (Wilson, 1996, quoted in Coakley, 2002). Another challenging question is: How does one explain the troubling prevalence of corruption, deviance, and crime among the privileged class and individuals who had opportunities to participate in high school or college sport, or even elite sport, throughout their youth and beyond?

Participation in sport is seen as a way of getting young people to internalize the values of conventionality and become better citizens, and there is evidence that sports, under the right circumstances, can contribute to the youth's moral development (Pennington, 2017). However, some studies have questioned the assumption that sports build moral character. Gamesmanship strategies, including cheating and aggression, are far from unheard of in youth sport. Many different types of aggressions (for example, physical, verbal, hostile, and instrumental) have been reported by high-school athletes who rationalized such behaviours as being part of the game (Camiré and Trudel, 2010). The findings of a study by Camiré and Trudel, who were interested in high-school athletes' perspectives on character development through sport participation, suggest that, 'while a combination of both social and moral values seems to be present, the majority of athletes tend to believe that the type of character that best describes the development that occurs in sport is social' (Camiré and Trudel, 2010: 205).

Gould and Carson also arrived at the conclusion that sport does not necessarily build character in youth: 'Sport participants are typically compared to non-participants on measures of moral development, with results often showing that participants do not exhibit higher levels of moral reasoning and, in some sports (e.g., male contact sports), may even exhibit lower levels of character development' (Gould and Carson, 2008: 63).

Many proponents of sport-based programmes, on the basis of some idealized beliefs in sport's capacity to promote moral development and character building, may be prepared to assume that engaging youth in sports will automatically serve the goals of education, socialization, and moral development (Hartmann and Kwauk, 2011). However, as Côté and Hancock (2016: 54) advised, '(s)port researchers and the wider sports community need to have a clear vision of the inherent value of sport participation and the best way to transmit positive personal values through sport'.

Positive contacts and role models

Some prevention programmes do not include youth participation in sports, but purport to expose youth to successful athletes as role models. An evaluation of a school-based programme that used successful sport personalities to deliver a series of motivational activities to young people revealed that, although the teachers and young people reported an immediate positive reaction to the activities, there was limited evidence of a wider impact on young people's behaviour, school attendance or self-esteem (Armour and Duncombe, 2012; Whatman and Main, 2018).

However, the majority of sport-based prevention programmes involved contacts and relationships with adults whom, for better or worse, youth may regard as role models. The actual impact of these role models on the youth's social, psychological, and human development is difficult to isolate from the impact of various other factors involved in a sport-based programme and is therefore rarely measured.

There is sometimes some confusion about the difference between adults acting as role models or as mentors. Mentoring is, of course, a very commonly used form of intervention with youth engaged in, or thought to be at risk for delinquent behaviour, school failure, aggression, or other antisocial behaviour. Adult–youth mentoring programmes are often a component of youth crime prevention programmes, whether related to sports activities or not, and they can have the desired impact (Tolan et al, 2013, 2016). The fact that sports activities can provide opportunities for developing positive mentorship is indisputable. But it is sometimes doubtful whether crime prevention outcomes should be attributed to the mentoring relationships or participation in sport.

Diversion

It is sometimes suggested that participation in sport can act as a *diversion* from crime and/or antisocial behaviour (Nichols, 1997), helping youth to avoid situations and activities that normally attract 'at-risk' youth (Crabbe et al, 2006). It is assumed that offering youth challenging and demanding activities that encourage them to channel their energy and quest for excitement into something worthwhile will divert these youth from offending. It is often suggested that the stimulus-seeking behaviour of certain types of delinquents explains why they may be attracted to and benefit from sports activities. The idea is that risky youth behaviour can be prevented by providing youth with alternatives and teaching them to make healthy decisions. Unfortunately, prevention programmes which pursue the general goal of diverting youth from crime by providing them with alternative leisure activities and a different social environment tend to have vague rationales and overly ambitious objectives or are based on fairly simplistic understandings of the multiple and complex causes of youth crime (Ehsani, Dehnavi, and Heidary, 2012).

The goal of some more structured interventions is to help youth 'become more intrinsically motivated by having goal-oriented leisure pursuits and decreasing levels of amotivation, learning to overcome peer pressure, and becoming more aware of leisure opportunities' (Caldwell and Smith, 2006: 411). Caldwell and Smith summarized, from a criminological perspective, the potential links between leisure and crime: (1) time filled with prosocial activities cannot be filled with deviant activities; (2) certain activities are more likely to instigate deviant behaviour or association with a deviant subculture; (3) time spent in informal and/or unsupervised activities is likely to promote deviance, while time spent in supervised activities protects against it; and (4) self-control and attachment to conventional norms and activities protect against deviant behaviour (Caldwell and Smith, 2006: 399).

Developmental outcomes

At the primary level of crime prevention interventions, sports programmes are seen as contributing, through an emotionally interactive engagement, to the development of personal skills or assets, including cognitive, social, emotional, and intellectual qualities, necessary to function constructively in society. The outcomes of youth sport involvement are sometimes referred to as the 3Ps: performance, participation, and personal development (Côté and Hancock, 2016). Peers and identity formation during sports activities (including the importance of being a team member, belonging to a team) have been shown to influence youth development (Andrews and Andrews, 2003; Bruner et al, 2017). However, it appears that sports activity's potential to promote youth's social engagement, and confer citizenship benefits, only materializes when the activity is integrated into wider programmes of social support and community engagement (Parker et al, 2019).

Other extra-curricular (after-school) activities can have a similar impact. Unstructured and structured after-school activities (sport and non-sport) provide contexts in which youth may face challenges and have positive and negative experiences that may benefit their development. What seems to matter the most is that the activity is one that they like and that engages them (Gadbois et al, 2019). Adventure education, for example, has also been shown to help youth to develop several life skills and contribute to their positive development (Ganea and Grosu, 2018). In fact, in recent studies of the benefits of extracurricular activities, sport was the only activity that showed both positive developmental outcomes (for example, the development of teamwork, emotional control, and initiative) and negative developmental outcomes (for example, pressure to do things that are morally wrong, or alcohol use).

Potentially misleading claims of developmental outcomes are sometimes made by various sports programmes. However, a growing number of studies might lead one to question the strong beliefs that often exist with regard to the developmental potential of sports (Coakley, 2011; Buelens et al, 2015). Assumptions made about how sports interventions contribute to achieving certain positive development outcomes and the ways through which these outcomes can be attained are seldom clearly formulated or left unquestioned (Coalter, 2013b). There is little understanding of the mechanisms through which sports can foster PYD (Buelens et al, 2015). The current evidence suggests that sport does not automatically promote healthy development and there is very little empirical evidence to suggest that sport participation itself is sufficient for healthy development. This has led some researchers to conclude that: 'There appears to be nothing inherent about playing, competing, or knocking a ball around that teaches adolescents positive values and skills' (Brunelle, Danish, and Forneris, 2007: 43).

On balance, research on the relationship between sport and youth development leads to the conclusion that the developmental outcomes are contingent on other factors and that, by itself, youth sport participation does not lead to regularly identifiable developmental outcomes. The assumption that sport can inherently transmit social values to participants has been successfully challenged. Producing PYD outcomes is contingent on a combination of many factors, including the type of sport played; one's peers, parents, coaches; and the norms and cultures associated with particular sports or sporting experiences. Coakley concluded that sport's developmental benefits are dependent on material and cultural contexts and may vary depending on, for example, the sport subculture, social relationships, shifting meanings of sport across the life course, and the social characteristics of participants (Coakley, 2011). Furthermore, as will be discussed in more detail later, it is often too quickly assumed that the learning that occurs during sport participation, including the values adopted and skills acquired, will necessarily be transferred to other non-sport contexts in a youth's life and automatically become resiliency factors.

Clearly, not all youth sports programmes are structured or implemented in a manner that supports youth development or the acquisition and transfer of key life skills to other life domains (Danish et al, 2004). For instance, researchers have pointed out that some youth sports programmes, instead of focusing on the short-term and inherent enjoyment that results from sport participation, focus too narrowly on performance, long-term athletic development, elitism, early selection, and early specialization with the explicit or implicit goal of developing elite-level athletes (Côté, Strachan, and Fraser-Thomas, 2008; Collins, 2010; Côté, Coakley, and Bruner, 2011). Some sports programmes organized and supervised by adults require higher levels of investment from earlier ages and focus on certain aspects of sport participation that do not necessarily coincide with children's motives to participate in sport in the first place (developing technical skills as opposed to simply having fun and being with friends) (Côté and Hancock, 2016).

There is evidence suggesting that sports programmes such as these may not provide optimal environments for youths' long-term participation in sport and may hinder physical and psychosocial development (Côté, Coakley, and Bruner, 2011). On the one hand, a sports programme solely focused on performance and the acquisition of technical skills neglects the importance of participation and personal development and minimizes the potential that sport involvement can have on youth's lives (Côté and Hancock, 2016). On the other hand, sports programmes that are primarily designed to teach life skills and personal development do not align necessarily with the youth's motivation to participate in sport (Côté and Hancock, 2016). However, when youth sports programmes incorporate the goal of holistic development of the athlete as a person, positive development outcomes will remain intact regardless of whether the athlete achieves great athletic success (Johnston, Harwood, and Minniti, 2013).

Life skills development

Given the progress achieved in the theory and practice of positive youth development (Waid and Uhrich, 2020), many researchers have focused their attention on better understanding how sport is conducive to the development of life skills. Life skills are skills that enable individuals to succeed in the different environments in which they live, such as school, work, home, and community. They are defined by the World Health Organization as 'abilities for adaptive and positive behaviour that enable individuals to deal effectively with the demands and challenges of everyday life' (World Health Organization, 1999). Life skills can be classified as behavioural (for example, effective communication), cognitive (for example, decision-making), interpersonal (for example, friendship, respect, teamwork), and intrapersonal (for example, focus, perseverance, goal setting, emotional regulation).

There is no doubt that youth have opportunities to learn social skills by participating in sports activities, including teamwork, leadership, communication, and learning to work with different types of people (Holt et al, 2008). There is also evidence that they can learn cognitive, emotional, and intellectual skills through sport, as well as agency, self-efficacy, goal setting, problem solving and time management. Under the right conditions sport can teach important life lessons to young people.

Pierce, Gould, and Camiré (2017) proposed the following definition of life skills development in sport:

> The ongoing process by which an individual further develops or learns and internalizes a personal asset (i.e., psychosocial skill, knowledge, disposition, identity construction, or transformation) in sport and then experiences personal change through the application of the asset in one or more life domains beyond the context where it was originally learned. (Pierce, Gould, and Camiré, 2017: 11)

The specific life skills that a particular sports programme is meant to help youth develop are often not specified (Gould and Carson, 2008: 59). Coaches in various sport contexts may focus on teaching different life skills. Many of them promote life skills based primarily on their own perception of the needs of the athletes, in both their sport and their personal lives (Trottier and Robitaille, 2014). Furthermore, life skills are only one important form of learning that take place in sport-based programmes (Ronkainen et al, 2021).

The acquisition of life skills is often considered as an end rather than as a means to an end. To date, research has carefully examined the acquisition of life skills, but has provided few insights about how the life skills acquired through the sport-based programmes play a role in changing participants' lives (Camiré et al, 2011). A comprehensive meta-analysis of randomized controlled trials on the effects of social skills training (not necessarily alone and not through sport) revealed that such interventions had a significant but small effect on aggression, delinquency, and related antisocial outcomes (Beelmann and Lösel, 2021). Unfortunately, the assumption that the acquisition or development of life skills prevents criminal involvement or desistance from crime, rather than simply resulting in producing more competent criminals, is on very shaky ground.

Life skills transfer

There is evidence, based on the youths' perceptions, that the life skills developed in high school sport are sometimes applied in other life domains (Kendellen and Camiré, 2017; Kendellen and Camiré, 2019). Surveys of sport participants about the skills they have acquired and the transfer of those skills to other contexts showed that participants are conscious of these skills (Bean, Kendellen, and Forneris, 2016). The ability to transfer skills learned in sports to other domains is a crucial aspect in achieving optimum personal development outcomes. To be considered life skills, the skills learned in sport must be transferable (Chinkov and Holt, 2016). Pierce and his colleagues proposed that 'for a skill learned in sport to qualify as a life skill, it must transfer and be successfully applied beyond sport' (Pierce et al, 2018: 11). Sport-based programmes can have a more sustained impact by focusing on the concepts of learning and 'skills transfer' (Armour and Sandford, 2013).

A central idea behind sport-based positive development programmes is that the learning that takes place during the sport-based programme will transfer valuable life skills to other non-sport contexts in a youth's life (Jacobs et al, 2017; Jacobs and Wright, 2018). However, claims that positive development outcomes are transferred to other domains should be made carefully (Vierimaa et al, 2012). In fact, there is no consensus regarding how life skills transfer from sport to other domains (Chinkov and Holt, 2016). Facilitating PYD through sport is not easy, nor is it automatic (Bean and Forneris, 2016). The life skills that are developed through sports programmes must be transferred beyond sporting domains. Any simplistic notion of learning 'transfer' should be questioned (Armour and Sandford, 2013).

Pierce, Gould, and Camiré (2017) explained that transfer is not an immediate outcome, but an ongoing process that occurs over time at the intersection of skill learning in one context and skill application in another context. They added that the potential for transfer resides within the learner, not the skill, and can occur in different ways depending on the individual's motivation, capacity, and personal characteristics. The individual is at the centre of the transfer process and must take advantage of opportunities to apply the skills acquired or perfected in sport in one or more life domains beyond sport. For these researchers, the process of life skills transfer is influenced by the specific transfer contexts (for example, classroom, peer group, community, family) that youth experience outside of sport and how athletes perceive and interpret these contexts (Pierce, Gould, and Camiré, 2017). Youth experience life skills transfer as an ongoing process whereby they continually interact with and interpret their environments (Pierce et al, 2018).

Studies that seek to understand the transfer process tend to focus on programmes with structured discussions around the topic, an established mentoring component, or complementary volunteer experience in the community (Jacobs and Wright, 2016). Unfortunately, less attention is given to what happens between the start of a programme and when a participant eventually makes use of life skills outside the programme (Jacobs and Wright, 2016).

Sport-based positive development programmes approach the question of skills transfer differently. Researchers have identified two approaches to the skill transfer question: the *explicit approach* and the *implicit approach* (Turnnidge and Hancock, 2014). The explicit approach proposes that youth who participate in sports need assistance in identifying the skills they can obtain through sport and understanding how these skills can be applied in other settings; they should be provided opportunities and strategies to practise their skills in a variety of contexts and develop the confidence to employ them in non-sport domains (Petitpas et al, 2005; Turnnidge, Côté, and Hancock, 2014). It is associated with sport programmes intentionally designed to provide instruction about the transferability of life skills, in which life skills sessions are often taught in non-competitive settings before, during, or after practices.

The implicit approach proposes that youth can be active producers of their own development and do not necessarily need to rely on adults in order to learn and apply transferable skills (youth-driven learning). This second approach places less emphasis on deliberately teaching the transfer of skills and more emphasis on offering sport environments that are conducive to youth-driven learning approaches (Turnnidge, Côté, and Hancock, 2014). However, both explicit and implicit means can be present within the same context and may combine to facilitate (or hinder) youth development within youth sport settings (Holt et al, 2012; Bean et al, 2018; Pierce, Erickson, and Dinu, 2019).

The explicit transfer approach is more widely supported in the youth sport literature (Camiré, Trudel, and Forneris, 2012; Camiré, Trudel, and Bernard, 2013; Weiss et al, 2013;

Bean et al, 2014). A qualitative study (18 youth, aged 12–13 participating in sport within the school context in the UK) suggested that the use of explicit strategies and group discussions aids the learning and transfer of life skills. For example, the Transfer-Ability Programme was a multifaceted intervention that sought explicitly to teach male participants life skills through sporting activities and facilitate transfer opportunities (Allen and Rhind, 2019).

Several studies have shown that an intentional focus on well-defined life skills within a sport-based youth development programme can promote a foundational understanding of life skills among youth (Hemphill, Gordon, and Wright, 2019). Intentionally structured programmes (that is, deliberately structured to teach life skills) scored higher on programme quality and PYD outcomes than non-intentionally structured programmes, with intentional sport scoring significantly higher on some measures of programme quality and PYD than leadership programmes (Bean and Forneris, 2016). Given that recent research emphasizes the crucial role of intentionality in maximizing the developmental gains of sport participation (Bean and Forneris, 2016; Holt et al, 2017; Bean et al, 2018), training for coaches can be designed to help them create environments conducive to the intentional teaching of life skills through high school sport (Camiré et al, 2020, 2021). When coaches use an intentional approach to youth development, they can play an important part in helping young people to reach adulthood with the necessary competencies to face the social challenges ahead (de Sousa Ferreira dos Santos et al, 2018).

There is still a lack of theoretical understanding of life skills transfer resulting from sport-based programmes (Holt et al, 2017) because the underlying mechanisms are very difficult to study (Jacobs and Wright, 2018, 2019). Participants may not be aware of the exact skill they have acquired, the behavioural change presumably associated with the skills transfer may not be immediately evident, the point at which a transfer takes place is hard to specify, or the transfer may only occur when an external factor provides an opportunity for the individual to try to apply the new skill (Jacobs and Wright, 2018, 2019).

Further research is required on the cognitive processes through which skills acquired by sport participation can be effectively transferred to other aspects of participants' life. However, research has recently begun to explain this transfer process and to identify programme features and delivery strategies that may aid such transfer, including creating conditions prior to the intervention that enhance transfer, mentoring, organizing peer discussions, providing opportunities for reflection after programme activities, and including follow-up experiences to enhance and reinforce learning. Many successful sport-based youth development programmes include follow-up activities, often in association with schools (Armour and Sandford, 2013; Armour, Sandford, and Duncombe, 2013; Eisman et al, 2018; Allen and Rhind, 2019), and purposefully seek to facilitate the transfer of life skills in collaboration with teachers and other school officials (Catalano et al, 2002; Armour and Sandford, 2013; Allen and Rhind, 2019). Opportunities for youth to discuss skills transfer with coaches and mentors are also important (Allen and Rhind, 2019). Additionally, providing youth with opportunities to get involved in further projects or complementary activities can also allow them to transfer the skills learnt through sport-based programmes to other situations and to develop them further (Armour, Sandford, and Duncombe, 2013).

Different strategies help youth identify and learn about life skills, including a specific life skills curriculum in the programme (Hodge et al, 2017) or requiring youth to memorize knowledge about life skills in order to provide youth with a common language around these skills and to foster a desire to apply them to their lives (Hemphill, Gordon, and Wright, 2019; Wright et al, 2020). These curricula are designed to help youth make cognitive connections about how life skills apply beyond the sport context and contribute to personal success or a better life.

Several studies have explored the role of athletic coaches in facilitating life skills transfer among youth through intentional teaching strategies. A pedagogical approach appears necessary, including a precise methodology with concrete aims alongside practical activities and strategies that make them work (Schwenzer et al, 2007). Jacobs and Wright (2016: 2) suggested that 'coaches must take advantage of authentic teachable moments that arise during practice to discuss how these experiences can be pertinent in other non-sport situations'. Trottier and Robitaille (2014) remarked that, by promoting self-confidence and self-awareness in athletes as a direct teaching strategy, coaches can create conditions that may help youth transfer their acquired life skills to other life areas (Trottier and Robitaille, 2014). Coaches must work deliberately to give youth the confidence to use the skills learned in sport in everyday life (Gould and Carson, 2008; Camiré, 2015).

Pierce and his colleagues identified seven strategies for coaches to help with life skills transfer: (1) prioritize coaching life skills and recognize the need to intentionally foster transfer; (2) foster life skills mastery and reinforce life skills transfer beyond sport; (3) maintain positive coach–athlete relationships; (4) expose young athletes to learning situations outside of sport to provide them with opportunities to apply their life skills; (5) develop partnerships and maintain open lines of communication with key social agents in athletes' lives at school, at home, or in the community; (6) provide life skills boosters; and (7) facilitate youth reflection (Pierce et al, 2018).

Coaches believe that they effectively teach life skills when they use specific pedagogical techniques to emphasize how skills learned in sport can transfer to other domains. These techniques include athletes sharing personal reflections, contracts for behavioural expectations, organizing team-bonding events, meeting with athletes individually, and goal setting (Camiré et al, 2011; Holt et al, 2012).

Finally, it seems that promoting the acquisition of life skills is not at all incompatible or unrelated to coaches' or athletes' performance enhancement goals. Many life skills learned in sport also help youth become better athletes and performers. Youth who apply life skills in non-sport contexts may refine these skills and learn not only to use them in life but also to transfer them back into the sport context (Pierce et al, 2018). Transferring life skills from sport to other life settings 'should not be seen as a separate activity unrelated to coaches or athletes' performance enhancement goals' (Pierce et al, 2018: 19). Performance success and PYD are goals of youth sport coaching that need not conflict with each other (Preston and Fraser-Thomas, 2018; Whitley, Massey, and Wilkinson, 2018).

Sport participation and social inclusion

Crime prevention most likely presupposes the *promotion of inclusion* and social cohesion, thus the idea that sport can play a unique role in this respect by generating social capital and by helping to mobilize communities and promote social inclusion and solidarity. Sport participation is often presented as a means of social inclusion and integration, as a site for meetings and bonding relationships between youth and formative role models (Eckholm, 2019). It offers youth a sense of belonging and an opportunity to expand their social networks (Catalano et al, 2002; Coalter, 2013; Roth and Brooks-Gunn, 2016; Bailey, 2018; Eisman et al, 2018). The need to create a sense of community and belonging among individuals has been identified by numerous authors as a significant element in any programme for disaffected youth (Sandford, Armour, and Warmington, 2006). Social capital is pivotal to understanding the impact of sport participation. It is viewed as a means of promoting social inclusion for marginalized groups (Sherry and Strybosch, 2012). Social capital theory assumes that 'social activity within the context of group participation, exhibiting clear aims and outcomes, results in an increase in the social capital for participants' (Sherry and Strybosch, 2012: 498). However, both the notions that sport and leisure activities are suitable means of promoting social relations and social capital and that social capital leads to social integration are disputable (Eckholm, 2019).

Expanding positive peer and adult connections is a mechanism by which organized activity participation may reduce risk of negative outcomes (Eisman et al, 2018). Morgan and Parker (2017), using the concepts of recognition and acceptance as a basis of social inclusion, suggested that within contexts in which youth can engage in meaningful and trusting interpersonal relationships with coaches and other key programme personnel, sport-based programmes may potentially 'incubate social assimilation' and promote integration.

Sport participation is also linked to the development of community resilience and the strengthening of cross-cultural awareness in young people and communities. For example, sport participation has the potential to facilitate the inclusion of migrants, but its effect is still limited by its role and the barriers that hinder the migrants' participation in sports (D'Angelo, 2019). An underlying assumption behind strategies to promote social inclusion through sports is that interactions between diverse social groups generate social capital, which can potentially function as a social lever for socially disadvantaged groups (Fehsenfeld, 2015). Sport participation may have potential social integration benefits by exposing participants to different cultural backgrounds and transforming attitudes and behaviours. Participation in sports can also improve feelings of confidence and self-esteem in relation to negotiating cultural differences and cultural stereotypes.

Sport participation does not always translate into genuine inclusion and there is still a lack of clear evidence to support the rhetoric about the ways in which sport can contribute to social inclusion (Dagkas, 2018). In reality, youth sport cultures are not always inclusive and sport programmes do not necessarily lead to greater social inclusion. Furthermore, vulnerable groups at risk of exclusion are not homogeneous. Each one presents peculiarities which should be considered at the time of intervention. To support the integration of at-risk groups, programmes must have an explicit commitment to support social integration and include interventions that are tailored to the needs and circumstances of the excluded group (Fernández-Gavira, Heute-García, and Velez Colon, 2017). Also, the strategies aiming at social inclusion through sports need to take social context and local power dynamics into consideration (Fehsenfeld, 2015).

Sport-based interventions have been developed as mechanisms through which social inclusion and social mobility can be promoted for marginalized youth. Sport-based programmes aimed at promoting social inclusion have a very limited impact on exclusionary processes and risk legitimating a reductive analysis of these complex processes, highlighting individual deficits and de-emphasizing structural inequalities (Kelly, 2011, 2012a and 2012b).

Another important way in which sport-based programmes may promote social inclusion is through interventions designed to sustain school engagement. Engagement or re-engagement with education and employment is a typical goal of sport-based programmes designed to enhance social inclusion of marginalized youth by helping them acquire psychological capital (Morgan and Bush, 2016; Morgan, Parker, and Roberts, 2019). Involvement in a community sport-based programme can potentially reconnect young people with formal education or, more specifically, enhance participants' sense of self-efficacy, hope, optimism, and resilience, and encourage them to see school engagement as a means to achieve their goals (Morgan, Parker, and Roberts, 2019: 1111). Sport-based community programmes for youth have the potential to help youth acquire human and social capital as a way to enhance employability prospects and, consequently, improve social mobility. The acquisition of positive psychological capital (that is, self-efficacy, hope, optimism, and resilience) is proposed to actualize social mobility (Morgan, 2017). However, it appears that sport-based programmes' impact on school engagement is very much context-specific and relates strongly to the youth's relationships with the facilitators (Sandford, Duncombe, and Armour, 2008). Morgan and Bush suggested that community-based sport coaches can become 'transformative leaders' and support schools in arresting school disengagement and reorienting young people from disadvantaged backgrounds towards more optimistic futures and educational objectives (Morgan and Bush, 2016).

Differential access to sport and exclusion

Social exclusion results in unequal access to educational, occupational, and political opportunity. Access to sport is indicative of wider social exclusion, as social marginalization and discrimination often result in lower access to and participation in sports (Sherry and Strybosch, 2012: 498). This includes access to sports facilities and spaces where access is restricted to certain groups, or where facilities are simply unavailable in low-resource areas. This problem is reflected in the fact that lower socio-economic populations tend to have lower rates of sport participation (Sherry and Strybosch, 2012).

Given increasing elitism, institutionalization, and competition in youth sport, youth sport programmes are not equally accessible to all youth, regardless of socio-economic status, race, culture, ethnicity, or gender (Fraser-Thomas, Côté, and Deakin, 2005). Vulnerable youth who might benefit most from sporting activities access them the least (Hallinberg et al, 2015). For example, children in care who, as a group, are at an elevated risk of victimization and criminal involvement, face specific challenges in accessing sport-based programmes, including disrupted patterns of engagement coupled with additional institutional constraints that shape access to sporting activities (Quarmby, 2014).

Participation in sports programmes is not always affordable to disadvantaged youth (Berdychevsky, Stodolska, and Shinew, 2022; Cameron and MacDougall, 2000). Availability of equipment, cost, transportation, and interest limit many youths' participation in after-school sports programmes. In addition to these limitations, safety concerns in urban communities also act as barriers to participation (Marttinen et al, 2019). Low neighbourhood safety and social disorder are related to decreased physical activity and participation in sports among youth. Street crime, gang activity, and fear can prevent youth from visiting parks or restrict their participation in sports activities (for example, going to places that require crossing gang boundaries) (Stodolksa, Shinew, and Acevedo, 2013).

Sport-based programmes need to address the obstacles to sport participation that confront various vulnerable groups (migrants, children of incarcerated parents, street children, gang-involved youth, Indigenous groups, and so on) and seek to engage youth and community members in the recruitment process, the choice of the sports activities, and the design of the programme (United Nations, 2020). For example, in Canada, Indigenous youth face multiple challenges accessing a sport system that is largely based on Euro-Canadian values and structures; they experience many constraints to participation, including racism, marginalization, and socioeconomic barriers (Strachan, McHugh, and Mason, 2018).

Planning sport-based interventions in a disadvantaged urban context or a remote location can present many challenges. Tensions within the community, rivalries, territorial conflicts between gangs, and a host of other factors and circumstances can negatively affect sport-based interventions. The social and power structures responsible for the exclusion of certain youth from healthy sports activities need to be considered.

THREE

Sports and Secondary Crime Prevention: Youth at Risk

At the secondary level of crime prevention, sport-based programmes have been relied upon to reach and support youth deemed 'at risk'. As discussed earlier, sport participation is mistakenly assumed to reform at-risk youth and prevent them from criminal involvement (Coakley, 2011; Eckholm, 2013; Riley et al, 2017). There is some evidence that sport can be an effective tool for recruiting and delivering other crime prevention interventions to mitigate risk factors and strengthen protective factors of crime and violence (Cameron and MacDougall, 2000; United Nations, 2020).

Many youth crime or drug prevention programmes use sports as a vehicle or platform for delivering various other forms of interventions. They are usually designed as early interventions to reduce the impact of risk factors and enhance corresponding protective factors, by targeting 'high risk' individuals or groups (Kelly, 2012a; 2012b). The nature and impact of these other interventions is sometimes unclear. The programmes may have many benefits for participants, but they tend to overstate their ability to prevent crime (Kelly, 2012b). The 'evidence' of their success, when there is any at all, is mostly anecdotal or based on the perceptions of participants or programme managers. Furthermore, many community-based programmes with limited funding focus on receptive youths and overemphasize the fact that these youth may somehow be 'at risk'.

Some of the programmes focus primarily on drug prevention. However, as Crabbe observed, sport is used in drug prevention and treatment interventions because young people enjoy it, but it is for the same reason that they might also choose to use illicit drugs or engage in criminal activity or sport-related violence (Crabbe, 2000). Moreover, the whole approach seems oblivious of the problem of doping and the use of performance enhancing drugs.

Spruit and her colleagues (2018b) evaluated a Dutch sport-based programme for youth at risk for juvenile delinquency. The primary outcome was juvenile delinquency, measured by official police data. The secondary outcomes were risk and protective factors for delinquency, assessed with self- and teacher reports. The study found small but significant intervention effects on juvenile delinquency, and no effects on the risk and protective factors of juvenile delinquency (Spruit et al, 2018b, 2018b). Another study based on youth's self-reported delinquent involvement (crimes against the person, crimes against property, and public disorder) at the beginning of their involvement in one of several sports programmes for at-risk youth and, again, six months later found significant reduction in self-reported delinquent behaviour (Khoury-Kassabri and Schneider, 2018).

Heller and her colleagues (2017), reporting on three large-scale randomized controlled trials in Chicago that tested interventions to reduce crime and school dropout by changing the decision making of economically disadvantaged youth (the Becoming a Man programme), concluded that it was very unlikely that sports activities were the main factor influencing outcomes. Cognitive changes (related to automatic thought processes) seem to have had the most impact, not changes in emotional intelligence or social skills, or self-control, or a generic mentoring effect.

It is increasingly recognized that when working towards broader prevention outcomes with youth at risk, especially socially vulnerable youth, a specific methodology is required

(Haudenhuyse, Theeboom, and Nols, 2012; Haudenhuyse, Theeboom, and Skille, 2014). Whether the intervention focuses on a psychological, a socio-pedagogical or a social capital approach, the method of intervention should be specified. Explicit and clearly articulated models of crime prevention are required to deliver interventions across multiple risk outcomes and support broader PYD outcomes (Allison et al, 2011).

Risk-based programming

As discussed in Chapter 1, there are several problems with a risk-based approach to crime prevention through sports. Risk prevention does not necessarily equate with successful adaptation or desistance from crime (Allison et al, 2011). However, risk prevention remains nonetheless at the centre of many crime prevention interventions, instead of more PYD strength-based approaches that build resilience.

The assumptions underlying many, if not most, sport-based crime prevention interventions are aligned with a deficit model of youth, which posits that young people from disadvantaged groups are uniformly deficient and in need of development, which can be achieved through sport (Coalter, 2010a, 2013; Coakley, 2011; Nols, Haudenhuyse, and Theeboom, 2017, 2017). These assumptions must also be challenged. The idea that young people from disadvantaged areas or background are uniformly deficient and in need of development is clearly problematic (Coalter, 2010a, 2013; Coakley, 2011; Nols, Haudenhuyse, and Theeboom, 2017). A study conducted in Belgium of 14- to 25-year-old participants in six sport for development programmes surveyed at two different points in time refuted the supposition that young people from disadvantaged urban areas are uniformly in need of more self-efficacy and self-esteem and showed that there was no change in the participants' development (Nols, Haudenhuyse, and Theeboom, 2017). Coalter (2013) cautioned against the 'dangers of an environmental determinism that assumes that deprived communities inevitably produce deficient people who can be perceived, via a deficit model, to be in need of "development" through sports'.

The approach is used to identify not only the risk factors but also the individuals to be targeted by various interventions. This typically leads to a very expansive definition of risk factors and, ultimately, the targeting and potential stigmatization of 'problem children' and their families (Garside, 2009). The approach tends to ignore underlying structural issues and inequalities. Crime is reduced to a putative individual social adaptation issue, and at-risk youth are deemed to be more inclined towards antisocial or criminal behaviour, whether because of their milieu, their uncaring or incompetent parents, or some other developmental deficit.

Research into risk factors associated with crime remains highly problematic; it is empirically very limited and theoretically ill-defined (Armstrong, 2004; Case and Haines, 2009, 2010). It is at the root of a 'sport as social control' approach which focuses on at-risk youth whom it characterizes as a danger or a threat to the community or in need of being controlled and socialized through sport or other structured activities (Chamberlain, 2013).

Risk of stigmatization and exclusion

Some efforts to target at-risk youth with sports programmes may serve to further stigmatize and isolate them from the community (Coakley, 2002; Armstrong, 2006; Coakley, 2011; Chamberlain, 2013; Eckholm, 2019). Sport-based crime prevention programmes designed for at-risk youth often target marginalized, disaffected youth, who can be difficult to locate and even more difficult to engage. Youth recruitment strategies, usually relying on sports clubs and volunteers, sometimes overlook young people whose social exclusion is more complex or acute, and who, most likely, are in greater need of intervention support. In fact, the social inclusion goals of some programmes are sometimes defeated by their own youth recruitment strategies or by predetermined participation targets which tend to exclude youth with more complex issues (Morgan and Costas Batlle, 2019).

The sports experiences of socially vulnerable youth are not always positive and supportive (Super et al, 2017). Sport participation can have integrative effects (friendship, trust, and social cohesion), but it can also entail the opposite (Collins and Kay, 2014, Bruner et al, 2016). For some socially vulnerable individuals, sport participation results in experiences of racism, or other forms of discrimination, bullying and exclusion, as well as feelings of rejection, disappointment, and personal failure. Although sport participation tends to be a positive experience for socially vulnerable youth, it can also instigate a 'negative spiral of vulnerability' (Super et al, 2019).

Sport-based crime prevention must safeguard participants. That includes ensuring non-discriminatory access for all to sports activities and access to safe sport spaces. It also includes making sure that interventions targeting at-risk groups or young offenders are trauma-informed and do not contribute to their stigmatization or social exclusion. Coaches can play a role in creating meaningful and supportive sporting experiences for vulnerable youth (Super, Verkooijen, and Koelen, 2018). With the right support, sports can provide participants with 'a strong motivation to reverse the downward spiral of vulnerability by providing a purpose or a direction in life' (Super et al, 2019: 29).

Finally, one needs to consider that sport clubs and organizations that support sport-based programmes are primarily interested in sport, and not necessarily in sport as a social service. There is perhaps an exaggerated belief in the interest of sports organizations in attracting and caring for socially excluded or deviant youth. As one author noted, 'projects desperate for money might pitch their idea at whichever scheme has money in whichever nomenclature or discourse required' (Groombridge, 2017: 138).

Given the various degrees of participation in and access to sport-based programmes by different populations, there is a need to develop strategies to engage those in vulnerable situations and with more restricted access. This includes devising effective recruitment strategies, conducting individual assessments to better understand the needs and aspirations of young participants, and ensuring the availability of and equitable access to sports facilities and spaces.

Strength-based programming: sport-based positive youth development

In view of the potentially stigmatizing effect of targeting individuals for interventions from various groups deemed to be at risk, flexible, individualized, strength-based approaches to programming should most likely be preferred to deficit-based approaches (United Nations, 2020). The PYD approach is based on a vision of positive adolescent development in which youth are regarded as a resource to be developed rather than a problem to be solved (Armour and Sandford, 2013). It can be defined as the 'development of personal skills or assets, including cognitive, social, emotional, and intellectual qualities necessary for youth to become successfully functioning members of society' (Weiss and Wiese-Bjornstal, 2009: 1).

Social responsibility[1] is also a goal of many physical activity based PYD programmes (Brunelle, Danish, and Forneris, 2007; Hellison, 2011; McDonough et al, 2013. That approach differs from others which focus on problems encountered by some young people while growing up (for example, learning disabilities, affective disorders, antisocial conduct, low motivation and achievement, substance abuse, poverty, and social exclusion) in that it focuses instead on the youths' talents, strengths, interests, and potentials (McDonough et al, 2013). The approach holds promise because it offers an alternative to the problem-centred or risk-mitigating vision of youth crime prevention that has dominated that field. In contrast to a traditional prevention perspective that focuses on mitigating certain risks, PYD emphasizes the resources relevant to promoting healthy development outcomes (Allison et al, 2011).

From a public safety perspective, the main drawback of the approach is that PYD has yet to be convincingly shown to prevent crime. For example, the evaluation of an intervention for young people displaying low-level antisocial behaviour in Chicago suggested that the intervention had its greatest impact on intermediate outcomes (for example, youth self-esteem and aspirations, or their behaviour at home or at school), but that these gains were not mirrored in the impact on the volume of offending behaviour, arrests, and use of drugs, alcohol, or other substances (Berry et al, 2009). The researchers remarked: 'In these areas, progress is much more hard won, and generally impacts are not statistically significant' (Berry et al, 2009: 71).

An evaluation in the UK of the Fairbridge Programme, which involved disadvantaged and disaffected young people in sport-based activities, was shown to increase the youths' personal and social skills in the short term (Astbury, Knight and Nichols, 2005). However, the gains in these skills did not appear to be maintained a year later, although they were still good predictors of long-term behavioural improvements. The supportive relationships with programme staff were of key importance in the long term. Initially, the nature of the sports activities was important in gaining involvement (Astbury, Knight and Nichols, 2005).

An evaluation of a sport-based life skills and community service programme indicated that the programme had a significant positive impact on adolescents' prosocial values and that the community service experience positively impacted the adolescents' levels of empathic concern and social responsibility (Brunelle, Danish, and Forneris, 2007). These findings support the view that 'sport can serve to enhance character and values when combined with life skill programming and the opportunity to engage in a sustained helping experience'

(Brunelle, Danish, and Forneris, 2007: 53). However, the enduring nature of that learning seems to depend on having the opportunity to put it into practice.

Another evaluation concerned a programme that used structured physical activity or sport as a vehicle for re-engaging disaffected youth and promoting positive personal and social development (a five-year, school-based programme for youth aged 13–14, involving outward bound activities and instructors). Researchers identified three crucial issues: the selection of participants; the 'transfer' of key skills; and the importance of positive social relationships (Armour et al, 2013). The study highlighted the importance of social and relational processes in physical activity programmes for disaffected youth. It also led to the conclusion that sport-based interventions are no panacea for social problems, nor can they expect to appeal to or influence every individual in the same way (Armour and Sandford, 2013; Armour, Sandford, and Duncombe, 2013). The lessons learned through this evaluation for future programme design were later summarised as follows:

> The impact of the program is highly individualized and context-specific in many cases, and that positive impact is more likely to be sustained when some or all of the following project features are in place: effective matching of pupil needs with the specific project objectives; locating project activities outside of the 'normal' school context; working closely with pupils to choose activities, set targets and review progress; establishing positive relationships between project leaders/supporters (mentors) and pupils; and giving pupils the opportunity to work with and for others. (Sandford et al, 2008: 419)

A central premise of PYD programmes aimed at crime prevention is the idea that promoting mastery of social and emotional core competencies[2] provides a connection between PYD and risk prevention programming. There is much speculation about the links between the so-called core competencies at the heart of PYD and youth violence or aggression (Sullivan et al, 2008). Much of that literature uses broad concepts such as aggression and externalizing behaviour, but since forms of violence differ in their aetiology, age of onset, and seriousness, the type of violence must be specified in discussions of the link between core competencies and violence (Sullivan et al, 2008).

School failure is understood as a risk factor for criminal involvement, and there is some evidence that the acquisition of core skills is linked to school performance and school attachment (Bradshaw et al, 2008). However, it appears that contextual factors at the level of the peer group, family, school, neighbourhood, and the physical environment moderate the influence of the core competencies on school success (Bradshaw et al, 2008).

Sport as a 'hook' for engaging youth

As Coakley suggested (1998: 102), it may be more useful to think of sport participation as a 'site for socialization experiences, instead of the cause of socialization outcomes'. One may remain critical towards the value of sports as a tool for youth development (Super et al, 2019). but there is no doubt that sport offers a 'hook' and a platform for various forms of individual and group interventions. Many adolescents participate in sports regardless of its prosocial value, and it makes perfect sense to create opportunities for prosocial development within an area of activity that occupies such a large proportion of the youth's time and thought (Scheithauer, Leppin, and Hess, 2020).

In sport-based programmes that include other interventions, such as teaching, mentoring, and other forms of individual support, the sports activity may not be of primary importance as long as it serves as a 'hook' for attracting youth into a stimulating field and engaging them in programmes where additional teaching or interventions are provided. Programme outcomes may be determined more by the strength of the non-sport aspects of the intervention than by the choice of sport or the extent of sport participation.

It is often suggested that desistance from crime and other crime reduction effects tend to occur when the initial contact with the sporting activity leads to deeper, more involved engagement giving rise to relationships of trust and acceptance with activity leaders and others. These relationships provide a platform upon which the development of the participant can be built, and which may lead to further opportunities in education, training, and employment (pathways that may deter or negate engagement in crime and antisocial behaviour). Research which examined the link between participation in sport-based programmes and desistance from crime highlighted the importance of strong interpersonal relationships between programme staff and the participants (Crabbe et al, 2006; Coalter, 2013b; Morgan and Parker, 2017). The assumption is that the positive trust-based relationships can contribute to development by enabling participants to feel valued or competent and enabling programme leaders to act as role models who can relate to the challenges faced by participants in their everyday life.

The type of sport

As Coalter noted (2012: 595), 'sport is a collective noun that hides more than it reveals'. Most of the literature on participatory sport-based programmes and crime prevention tends to focus on a few team-based competitive sports (for example, football, rugby, basketball, hockey) or combat sports (for example boxing, mixed martial arts). Other sports are occasionally mentioned, including golf (Weiss et al, 2013; Weiss, Bolter, and Kipp, 2016; Kendellen et al, 2017), running, circus arts programmes (Smith et al, 2017; Agans et al, 2019), canoeing, weightlifting, wilderness adventure (Ganea and Grosu, 2018), indoor competition climbing programmes (Garst, Stone, and Gagnon, 2016), or parkour (Gilchrist and Wheaton, 2011; Herrmann, 2016; Gilchrist and Osborn, 2017). All of them can be intentionally structured to teach life skills or linked to life-skills training activities. For example, circus arts programmes emphasize building challenging physical skills but with an artistic rather than a competitive orientation. According to one study, participants in youth circus programmes demonstrated significant growth in social and emotional skills over the course of their programme participation (Agans et al, 2019). With the right context and careful and intentional programming, it seems that any sport or physical activity can be used as a platform for crime prevention programming.

Different forms of participation can also provide a worthwhile platform for youth development. Opportunities to volunteer or participate in different capacities (as a member of the coaching team, as a referee, and so on) in a sport-based programme can help to recruit youth who would otherwise not be interested in joining a programme. This highlights the importance of providing experiences of success through volunteering as well as the importance of there being a gradual take-up of responsibilities, thereby increasing adolescents' engagement at their own pace (Buelens et al, 2017). A systematic approach of the volunteer training programme can play an important role in developing the competencies of socially vulnerable youth (Buelens et al, 2015).

As one of the coaches interviewed during the consultation conducted during our own study put it:

'There is no question that youth will learn things from their sport experience, no matter what sport. But what is it they are learning: that they are not good enough to get some ice time, that others excel because they break the rules, that winning is the only thing that matters? How the sport is practiced is probably more important than the choice of sport.'

Youth psychosocial experiences in sport-based physical activities vary based on activity characteristics (Evans et al, 2017). Programme activities should have an element of thrill and excitement since many of the youth involved may need greater amounts of stimulation to become motivated (Andrews and Andrews, 2003). However, experts have also suggested that sports activities which de-emphasize regulations and winning, and instead emphasize choices for participants and the tailoring of interventions to meet individual needs, are better at providing a platform for crime prevention interventions (United Nations, 2020).

There is also a concern that the use of unsuitable sports may have a detrimental effect. The use of combat sports or martial arts as a basis for crime prevention interventions remains quite controversial. Does combat sport have an impact on participants' criminality and, if so, are combat sports appropriate for use in crime prevention strategies or, for that matter, in offender rehabilitation programmes?

Ten years ago, a review of the considerable amount of research conducted over the previous two decades on the social-psychological outcomes of martial arts involvement, with youth in particular, did not provide overall conclusive evidence regarding these outcomes (Vertonghen and Theeboom, 2010). A few studies reported negative outcomes as a result of martial arts involvement, such as increased antisocial behaviour, although the bulk of the research 'mostly pointed in the direction of the appearance of positive effects, going from a higher level of self-regulation and an increased psychological well-being, to a decreased violence level among its participants' (Vertonghen and Theeboom, 2010: 534).

Over the years, the practice of martial arts, increasingly popular among youth, raised concerns because of the possible harmful effects on the personal and social well-being of participants in terms of aggressive and violent behaviour (externalizing behaviour). It is unclear whether martial arts participation is associated with externalizing behaviour, but a meta-analysis of 12 studies revealed that there was no relation between martial arts participation and externalizing behaviour in youth (Gubbles et al, 2016). As compared to non-athletes and team sport athletes, martial arts participants showed similar levels of externalizing behaviour, but they showed more externalizing behaviour when compared to individual sport athletes (Gubbles et al, 2016). Another meta-analysis of 12 studies measuring the impact of martial arts on problematic externalizing behaviour (aggression, anger, and violence) among youth aged 6 to 18 concluded that martial arts have a potential to reduce externalizing behaviours in youth (Harwood, Lavidor, and Rassovsky, 2017). It has been suggested that combat sport participation can act as a protective factor which distances participants from socio-cultural and individual risk factors in the behavioural, economic, and social spheres (Jenkins and Ellis, 2011). However, it appears that martial arts intervention programmes that focus exclusively on playing the sport or teaching moral lessons do not produce the desired reduction in aggressive behaviour outcomes (Lai Chu Fung et al, 2018).

On the one hand, integrating youth into supportive martial arts communities provides opportunities for mentorship, the development of external and internal assets, and youth psychosocial development (Lorenz, 2018). Martial arts may have the potential to reduce externalizing behaviours in youth, although research is needed to determine the mechanisms of change and specify the most relevant population groups for targeted interventions (Harwood, Lavidor, and Rassovsky, 2017). On the other hand, the values learned through martial arts are not exclusively prosocial. Many of them are problematic expressions of masculinity (for example, toxic masculinity): fear is constant in mixed martial arts (MMA) and part of establishing one's masculine identity consists of learning to manage one's fears and fostering fear in others, or managing one's emotional manhood (Vaccaro, Schrock, and McCabe, 2011). Also, MMA participants often refer to the potential of violence in everyday life as a reason for practising MMA to learn how to respond to violent threats in the cage or on the street (Green, 2016).

At yet another level, gyms (both public and private) often play a role in the recruitment strategies of far-right extremist groups. Miller-Idriss (2020) notes how extreme right-wing martial arts gyms in Germany have long sought to integrate physical fitness, militancy, and extreme nationalist ideologies. She also notes the convergence of various studies linking masculinity and sports. She writes: 'MMA becomes a powerful incubator for the far right when these ideas about masculinity – the notion that being a man is achieved through violent confrontation, domination, and physical intimidation of opponents – layered onto far-right ideology about immigrant invasions and defense of the nation' (Miller-Idriss, 2020: 106).

Relationships and the role of coaches and facilitators

One of the objectives of sport-based programmes is to support positive interactions between the youth and key social agents (peers, parents, coaches, leaders, teachers). As will be further discussed in Chapter 7, facilitators, sport coaches, and volunteers play a crucial role in the successful delivery of sport-based crime prevention interventions, by recruiting and motivating youth, providing role models, developing mentoring relationships, keeping the youth engaged in the programme, and providing a safe and supportive environment.

The development of authentic and meaningful relationships between coaches and youth, based on trust and mutual respect, is a key aspect of these sport-based crime prevention interventions. Both the behaviour of coaches, mentors, and programme leaders and their relationship with programme participants have been shown to be extremely important (Crabbe, 2000; Coakley, 2011; Coalter, 2013a). Supportive relationships seem to have most impact on long term results (Astbury, Knight, and Nichols, 2005; Sandford, Duncombe, and Armour, 2008; Coalter, 2013a). Research has stressed the importance of relationships between practitioners and participants in sport-for-development programmes and the importance of trust and respect in these relationships (Debognies et al, 2019).

Several sport-based programmes are sponsored by or led by police organizations as part of efforts aimed at strengthening community–police relations.[3] This kind of police engagement in sport-based programmes takes many forms, including as part of community policing initiatives, and aims to improve police–community relations and youth's respect for the law.

FOUR

Sports and Tertiary Crime Prevention: Desistance from Crime

At the tertiary level of crime prevention, the goal of interventions is to prevent recidivism or support desistance from crime. In that context, sport-based programmes either in the community or in a correctional setting are sometimes proposed as a means to contribute to the rehabilitation and reintegration of offenders. However, there are still very few such programmes for young offenders, whether in the community or in institutions. For instance, there was not a single sport-based programme for convicted young offenders among those we reviewed in British Columbia.

Despite the fact that sport-based programmes targeting known young offenders remain a rarity and that their crime prevention outcomes have never been properly evaluated, these programmes have nevertheless been declared 'promising' (Meek, 2020). Without necessarily disputing that premature conclusion, it is important to realize that the promise in question remains largely theoretical. Some preliminary research has attempted to link sport-based interventions and offenders' desistance from crime. However, at this point, the effectiveness of rehabilitation efforts through sport remains uncertain (Meek, 2012, 2014, 2018; Meek, Champion, and Klier, 2012; Lewis and Meek, 2012; Gallant, Sherry, and Nicholson, 2015; Meek and Lewis, 2014a, 2014b; Parker, Meek, and Lewis, 2014; Sempé, 2018; Psychou et al, 2019). There are still many unanswered questions around whether these sport-based crime prevention programmes (whether administered in the system or in the community) can aid in desistance from crime and how this process works.

Supporting desistance

It is important to understand the process of change that tertiary crime prevention programmes are trying to support. That process is perhaps best described as 'desistance from crime'. The importance of understanding that process is well recognized within criminal career research which tries to account for the onset of, maintenance of, and desistance from criminal behaviour. However, despite its importance to the criminal career paradigm, desistance is relatively understudied in criminology (Lussier, McCuish, and Corrado, 2015).

Several desistance studies are relevant to the topic of sports and crime prevention. The best-known among them was Laub and Sampson's (2003) ground-breaking multiple-wave longitudinal study on 500 male delinquents from Boston. The study was based on an impressive dataset that stretched over 40 years, with interviews conducted at various points throughout many of the offenders' lives. One of their main findings was that most offenders go through a gradual process of desistance in which offending is greatly reduced because of various personal and institutional controls (for example, becoming involved with structured activities, getting a good job, or becoming a parent) and the stake in conformity that results from having a network of relationships and social bonds. Their findings also indicated that desistance was the norm even for very serious and persistent offenders.

Other researchers noted that many desistance studies make use of data from samples of general and at-risk youth drawn from middle and high schools and that these school-based samples include very few chronic juvenile offenders, young murderers, gang members, or juvenile sex offenders (Lussier, McCuish, and Corrado, 2015: 88). For that reason, the conceptualization of desistance as the result of a maturational process may not be generalizable to violent and sex-offending sub-groups (Lussier, Corrado, and McCuish, 2016). Lussier and his associates (Lussier, McCuish, and Corrado, 2015; Lussier, Corrado, and McCuish, 2016) conducted a longitudinal study of 349 incarcerated juvenile offenders between the ages of 12 and 23 to better understand the desistance process for serious young offenders. Using several modelling strategies to understand different offending trajectories, they found that most of the individuals were not on a life-course pattern of violent and sexual offending, but rather were at different stages of desistance; desistance was relatively bounded to onset and level of offending. They also observed a deceleration of offending preceding desistance, a process during which offenders gradually stop committing crime because of negative life consequences associated with legal sanctions or physical injuries that occur during or as a result of the commission of the crime (Lussier, McCuish, and Corrado, 2015). Their findings suggest that the various conceptualizations of desistance are not necessarily contradictory but capture distinct aspects of the same underlying process.

Contemporary research on desistance indicates that most offenders desist (even the most serious ones) and that they often exhibit a zigzag pattern of offending in which they gradually drift away from crime (Lussier, McCuish, and Corrado, 2015). Some research suggests that a 'knifing off' process, a process of reinventing oneself – or identity reconstruction – that is often triggered by a change in life circumstances, may be very important to understanding this sporadic pattern of offending (Laub and Sampson, 2001 and 2003; Maruna and Roy, 2007). Maruna and Roy (2007) argue that researchers must consider how both legitimate and criminal opportunities may be affected by the knifing off process (for example, imprisonment may knife off criminal and future employment opportunities).

Another desistance study which provided insights for the prevention of recidivism among young offenders was conducted by Amemiya, Kieta, and Monahan et al (2017). After interviewing 39 males (median age 17 years old) about their reflections on desistance from crime, researchers identified four key themes about the subjects' motivation to end their criminal career. The four themes were: experiencing a psychological reorientation; reacting to consequences associated with committing crime (for example, physical injury or criminal justice punishment); viewing themselves as persistently stuck in a criminal lifestyle; and being in the wrong place at the wrong time (that is, they were unlucky and do not normally offend or get in trouble). The subjects mentioned five ways in which they asserted their agency to support their own desistance from crime: establishing strong relationships; managing peer groups; working for long-term goals; structuring activities; and avoiding trouble and criminal opportunities. Participation in sports was mentioned by respondents as one of several types of structuring activities that could lead to desistance.

Summarizing previous research, Lussier and his colleagues (2015) observed that desistance from crime has been conceptualized in four ways: as an event; in probabilistic terms; as a process; and bounded to specific offending trajectories. Increasingly, there has been a shift towards reconceptualization of desistance from deviance from a static event to a developmental process, redirecting attention to the cognitive transformation associated with desistance (Laub and Sampson, 2003; Farrall, 2019). Viewing desistance as a process involves examining the factors and mechanisms associated with the transition to law-abiding behaviour (Lussier, McCuish, and Corrado, 2015: 91).

From that perspective, desistance is a process of cognitive transformation or change in identity whereby individuals stop identifying as 'offenders' and craft non-offender identities. Desistance research emphasizes that offenders identify a future self that aids desistance efforts. Hunter and Farrall (2018) described the role of future selves in desistance, outlining how a conception of oneself as a non–offender assists efforts to refrain from offending.

Most studies draw a connection between individuals' identities and their motivations for behaviour. A shift towards a new identity is seen as playing a central role in almost all recent studies of desistance (Villeneuve et al, 2021), a step in a journey towards social inclusion or social reintegration. That shift is usually conceptualized as the result of a successful but not necessarily linear process during which various experiences lead to cognitive transformations, identity changes, and lifestyle adjustments. The shift can either be facilitated or hindered by individual agency, social support, or structural opportunities for change. The more entrenched an offending career has become, the more significant are the changes required to the individual's core identity (Farrall, 2019: 22).

Cognitive processes are necessary but not always sufficient to provide a path to sustained behavioural change. Access to opportunities to change and develop is crucial to desistance. Moreover, desistance research consistently shows that social relations have a role to play in variously constraining, enabling, and sustaining desistance (Weaver, 2017). The desistance process is complicated by ambivalence about change, and social-relational support is therefore critical. The role of wider relational factors in supporting the desistance process is essential (McNeill, 2006). Social capital, defined as the resources that reside in social networks and social relationships, is seen as an important contributing factor.

Wider relational factors can 'cement' the desistance process (Albertson and Hall, 2020: 313). Changes in social networks and relational dynamics, including changes in relationships/supports from parents and affiliation with delinquent peers, play a significant role in the change processes (Copp et al, 2020). The sense of belonging to a moral and political community or being accepted within a different social network can consolidate the behavioural changes and the shift to a non-offending identity (McNeill, 2006).

From a practical point of view, considering desistance as a social-relational process raises questions about how that process can be facilitated by various forms of assistance, including specific programmes. Even if desistance is understood to happen naturally, it does not mean that it cannot be assisted or accelerated (McNeill, 2021; Johnson and Maruna, 2020). In fact, there are many ways in which the desistance process can be assisted. As McNeill takes care to explain:

> For example, desistance is linked to physical and psychological maturation, but we should understand this not just as a spontaneous and inevitable process associated with ageing, but also as a social process which can be enabled or impeded by a person's associates and environments. Similarly, desistance is often linked to the development of new social bonds like those associated with intimate relationships, parenthood, or employment; but it should be obvious that we find our ways into these important connections not entirely by accident. More often, they reflect supported changes in our social positions. (McNeill, 2021: 35)

Jump (2021), who studied the role that boxing may have played in supporting identity reconstruction and desistance from crime among young males, suggested that:

> A critical feature of desistance is finding an activity or change in circumstances that has the potential to engage and motivate individuals and enable them to develop alternative pro-social identities, as well as contributing to the development of positive networks. The key to understanding desistance in this context, is the recognition that in order to abstain successfully from crime, offenders need to 'make sense' of their lives as non-offenders. The desistance literature has identified a range of factors associated with no longer being actively

involved in offending, many of which are concerned with the acquisition of something meaningful to the offender which promotes a re-evaluation of their sense of self. (Jump, 2017: 1098)

More fundamentally, when considering how best to support youth desistance from crime, as Deuchar and his colleagues insist, 'it is important to recognize the complex nature of this change process' (Deuchar et al, 2016: 726). Bearing in mind that desistance is often best described as a work-in-progress and that turning points are a salient feature of the desistance process, the role that sport might play in stimulating and supporting change needs to be more fully articulated (Carlsson, 2013).

At this point, unfortunately, a lot more is known today about the desistance process than about the kind of interventions or programmes that can actually support it. The latter knowledge is very limited and unstructured (F.-Dufour, Villeneuve, and Peron, 2018: 229), but a few programmes are worth mentioning.

Sport-based programmes for gang-involved youth

Some sport-based crime prevention interventions are designed more specifically to support *gang prevention* initiatives and aim to prevent the recruitment of at-risk youth into gangs, to offer gang-involved youth a way out, or to facilitate their social reintegration. Sport-based interventions are meant to create opportunities to engage gang-involved youth in positive transitional experiences, alternative identity construction, and desistance actions (Osterberg, 2020). Programmes addressing youth gang involvement that include recreation components create opportunities for them to develop prosocial relationships with their peers and help to break racial/ethnic stereotypes (Berdychevsky, Stodolska, and Shinew, 2022). Unfortunately, as relational analysis studies and studies of co-offending have shown (Boivin and Morselli, 2016), sports activities, like any other social activity, can also present opportunities for young people to develop or diversify their criminal social capital and form or join delinquent networks.

Some interventions are potentially more effective than others in reducing youth violence and gang involvement. For example, a small study of sport-based interventions and self-reported gang involvement and delinquency among a diverse sample of rural high school girls reported less gang involvement and lower individual delinquency (Taylor et al, 2016). Interventions addressing gang involvement can help youth develop prosocial relationships with their peers and 'give youth a sense of purpose and ownership that can keep them on track in their often chaotic and unfulfilling environments' (Berdychevsky, Stodolska, and Shinew, 2022: 360). It also tends to be accepted that sports and other forms of recreation can be part of a comprehensive and balanced combination of approaches, or a 'weed and seed' strategy blending suppression, enforcement, prevention, intervention, and rehabilitation goals (National Gang Center, 2010).

An ethnographic study conducted in a boxing rehabilitation centre on the outskirts of Copenhagen, Denmark, suggested that boxing can offer disadvantaged minority male gang members an opportunity for alternative identity construction and support their progressive desistance from gangs (Deuchar et al, 2016). Deuchar and colleagues (2016) explained that desistance is not just about transformations in offenders' circumstances, but also involves subjective and intersubjective processes such as individuals' reconstructions of identities. They noted that the rehabilitation programme provided ethnic minority male gang members who had become stigmatized by the criminal justice system with a safe space to perform broader versions of locally dominated views on masculinity and to reflect on their current situations and dilemmas. The study aimed to identify strategies that may help to support young males, caught in the 'double binds related to territoriality and gang conflicts', to transition towards criminal desistance (Deuchar et al, 2016: 729). It explored how stigmatized and socially excluded young ethnic minority Danes could draw upon boxing to reposition themselves and construct reformed masculine positions in relation to multiple overlapping social domains (Deuchar et al, 2016: 738).

> Since boxing has been described as the 'manly art' and some evidence suggests that it provides working-class young men with a highly respected means of crafting the body into physical capital while also providing a socially accepted context for channelling aggression and re-building social status, it provided us with the ideal context for exploring the links between transitional masculinity and desistance. (Deuchar et al, 2016: 738)

Although its outcomes in terms of desistance from crime were modest, the programme showed that sport-based interventions that are framed within a hegemonic masculine narrative can help disadvantaged young men develop the resilience and perseverance needed to overcome social stigma and to find a path towards desistance.

Another issue sometimes raised concerning interventions with gang-involved youth is whether group interventions are possible or advisable when working with co-offending individuals. At this point the evidence is far too thin to answer the question conclusively. However, recent work suggests that despite negative presumptions about co-offender interactions, co-desistance scenarios are possible. The concept of co-desistance – defined as the movement towards the cessation of offending by groups of persons known to have frequently offended together – reverses current risk presumptions around co-offender interactions and instead warrants using co-offenders' social bonds to forge collective pathways out of crime (Halsey and Mizzi, 2022: 12). The experience of group loyalty, adherence to a code, and mutual support among participants may carry over from their former situation to the new one (Halsey and Mizzi, 2022: 14).

Sport-based programmes in correctional settings

There is no reason why sport-based programmes for young offenders should be offered only in correctional settings. No one would seriously suggest that offenders should be sent to prison so that they may benefit from sports activities. In practice, however, at this tertiary level of intervention, most sport-based programmes take place in prison or detention facilities and are rarely followed by other interventions post-release. In some instances, young offenders can access or are referred to existing community-based programmes designed more generally for at-risk youth. It also stands to reason that designing sport-based programmes for young offenders in the community could emphasize their contacts with the justice system and contribute to their further stigmatization and make their social reintegration even more challenging than it already is (McAra and McVie, 2009).

The European Prison Rules stipulate the right of prisoners to have access to sports activities (Council of Europe, 2006). Rule 4 of the United Nations Standard Minimum Rules for the Treatment of Prisoners (the Nelson Mandela Rules) (United Nations, 2015) requires prison authorities to offer, delivered in line with the individual treatment needs of prisoners, 'education, vocational training and work, as well as other forms of assistance that are appropriate and available, including those of a remedial, moral, spiritual, social and health- and sports-based nature'.

There are various benefits from practising sports or other physical activities in prison: improved physical health and psychological functioning; relief from boredom; alleviation of stress, depression, and anxiety. Performing sports activities can be a coping mechanism for inmates to combat mental and emotional distress. Sport and recreation programmes appear to have a positive influence on inmates' health and behaviour. Yoga, for example, is used to increase one's sense of well-being in prison (Muirhead and Fortune, 2016; Wimberly and Engstrom, 2018; Bartels, Oxman, and Hopkins, 2019).

There is only scant research on the impact and significance of sports activities in correctional environments (Norman, 2017; Norman and Andrews, 2019). Research typically identifies three aims of prison-based sport programmes: inmate health and well-being, inmate rehabilitation, and inmate management. In practice, most programmes tend to focus on prisoners' health and well-being, and inmate management; preventing reoffending, as an expected outcome, tends to be an afterthought or, at best, a residual effect (Gallant, Sherry, and Nicholson, 2015; Woods, Breslin, and Hassan, 2017). In most countries, sport in prison occupies a solely recreational role, but in some countries, it is also considered a form of education (Martos-García, Devís-Devís, and Sparkes, 2009). According to Norman (2017: 600), 'the rationale underpinning such interventions is commonly based upon a faulty assumption that sport can inherently transmit social values, such as hard work, discipline, and respect for authority, to its participants'.

In prison, sport-based programmes may create an opportunity for staff and community partners to engage with especially hard-to-reach prisoners and develop positive support and mentoring relationships with them (Meek, 2012). Unfortunately, there are also barriers to sports activities in prison, both internal (for example, lack of motivation, lack of self-efficacy, low energy, and age) and external to the individual (for example, lack of resources, lack of access or lack of age-appropriate opportunities) (Brosens et al, 2017).

The environment in which a sport-based prevention programme is delivered obviously matters and the correctional environment offers some serious challenges. Can sport-based programmes support youth positive development while they are detained in a correctional facility? Research shows that 'seeking and supporting changes in behaviour depends on and is secured by actively developing the institutional climates and cultures, and the social relations and contexts, within which people are enabled to flourish. Absent these systemic and social preconditions, efforts to reduce reoffending are insecure at best' (McNeill, 2021: 37).

Studies indicate that sport within youth institutional settings can be beneficial (for example, learning social skills) (Amtmann and Kukay, 2016) or problematic (for example, leading to social exclusion), depending on how these activities are structured, delivered, and, ultimately, experienced by the youth. Sports can play a role in the rehabilitation of youth in detention, but should be used selectively (Andrews and Andrews, 2003; Williams et al, 2015; Woods, Breslin, and Hassan, 2017a, 2017b; Roe, Hugo, and Larsson, 2019). According to Andrews and Andrews (2003), unsuitable activities and programmes may have a detrimental effect on participants. Some sports, because of their structure, context, and rules, replicate institutional settings from which these youths are already alienated, and this may be problematic for some youth.

Meek, who reviewed the use of sport to promote employment, education, and desistance from crime in English and Welsh prisons, concluded that 'although sport is not the only answer, it can provide some solutions to the long-standing problems of the disengagement, disempowerment, and disaffection of people in prison' (Meek, 2020: 410). Many of the programmes she reviewed were the result of partnerships between prisons, and community groups and clubs. Their relevance to individual desistance from crime, especially among those attempting to leave behind a past which may have involved gang-related offending, was that they sometimes provided access to a prosocial network and positive role models, and the opportunity to gain new experiences and achievements (Meek, 2014). In sum, Meek adds, 'participating in sport can offer an alternative to offending which not only has intrinsic value but also provides a relatively easy way to establish a more positive self-identity' (Meek, 2020: 411).

Since desistance is best understood as a gradual process – a 'drifting', involving progression and relapse – that process for young men is 'imbued with age-specific norms of what it means to "be a man" and successfully do masculinity in different stages of life' (Carlsson, 2013: 686). One important way of helping young males to desist from crime is to engage them in discussions of norms, adulthood, and masculinity, and to provide them with resources –cognitive and material –for coping with them (Carlsson, 2013).

Correctional institutions may be able to support individuals' move away from criminal careers by engaging their masculinity (Søgaard et al, 2016: 100). A study of the New Start programme involving boxing showed how a correctional sport-based and mentoring programme can utilize hyper-masculine symbolism and imaginaries to encourage young offenders and drug abusers to engage in narrative reconstructions of identities and to socialize participants into new subject positions defined by agency, self-responsibility, and behavioural changes (Søgaard et al, 2016). During interviews the young men expressed 'ideals and values such as agency, fight, responsibility, self-control, independence and determinedness when describing how they saw their own process of desistance', while they presented desistance from crime as 'a road full of obstacles, trials and temptations, taking determination and will, and not something everybody could do' (Søgaard et al, 2016: 108).

The authors summarized some of their findings as follows:

> Our findings suggest that one reason why many of the young men seemed to accept the New Start programme and its strategic masculinization of desistance was that it drew on but also redirected the expression of many of the same masculine values, such as individual will-power, autonomy and the ability to 'man up' to challenges, which had also been central to the young men's former street-cultures. In the analysis we

demonstrated how institutional discourses conveying values of agency and individual responsibility both informed and were negotiated in the young men's narrative attempts to reformulate masculinity identities. (Søgaard et al, 2016: 115)

An attempt at system-wide integration of sport in youth crime prevention

In Thailand the Department of Juvenile Observation and Protection in the Ministry of Justice works in partnership with several non-governmental organizations and the private sector to provide seamless support for juveniles to advance their skills, rebuild their lives, and reintegrate into societies. Most notable is 'Bounce Be Good', or the BBG Sport Club, under the initiative of Her Royal Highness Princess Bajrakitiyabha. The BBG Sport Club presently operates in five provinces of Thailand. The Club works closely with the Department of Juvenile Observation and Protection in the Ministry of Justice, and the Department of Children and Youth in the Ministry of Social Development and Human Security. The initiative also builds on partnerships with community-based organizations including, for example, the Badminton Association of Thailand and the Table Tennis Association of Thailand (Thailand Institute of Justice, 2019). The initiative is presently under evaluation.

The main mission of the BBG Sport Club is to promote the rehabilitation of youth involved, or at risk of getting involved, in crime by building on the passion for sports and creating sport participation opportunities for underprivileged children and youth 'who have chosen the wrong path'. The prospect of a career in sport is used also as a motivating factor. Since its creation in 2016, more than 370 children and youth participated in the programme and, according to programme monitoring data, none of them has reoffended or 'fallen into the cycle of violence'.

Impact on social reintegration

In the UK, an evaluation of a sport-based (rugby and football) programme in prison to help young adult male prisoners in identifying and meeting resettlement needs and facilitating their transition from custody to community showed that it had motivated individuals to take responsibility for their actions and inspired them to generate positive aspirations for the future. The study confirmed that statistically significant improvements were observed in established measures of conflict resolution, aggression, impulsivity, and attitudes towards offending, following participation (Meek, 2012).

A football and rugby initiative, consisting of offering four consecutive sports academies delivered to 79 young men serving a prison sentence in England, were evaluated (Meek, 2014). The sport academies, each of three to four months' duration, were delivered in prison and consisted of intensive football or rugby coaching, training, and matches alongside classroom-based exercises focusing on core life skills, as well as support in social reintegration planning. According to the evaluator:

> Observed changes in a spectrum of self-report psychometric measures from baseline (Time 1) to completion of the programme (Time 2) and at longitudinal follow-up (Time 3) were used to assess changes in attitudes and behaviours, with sustained improvements shown on measures of aggression, impulsive behaviours, attitudes towards offending and conflict resolution skills. (Meek, 2014: 89)

A reconviction rate of 21 per cent was observed among the 42 programme participants who had been released from prison one year after release. Having acknowledged the various limitations of her study, Meek nevertheless concluded that it provided 'much needed evidence on the efficacy of using sport as a mechanism to engage young prisoners in holistic resettlement programmes' (Meek, 2014: 103).

An evaluation of a 12-week programme intended for child and youth sexual offenders and combining boxing and cognitive behavioural therapy in South Africa (Fight with Insight) concluded that it seemed to have an impact on recidivism and interpersonal relationships, although the effect may be attributable mostly to the therapy (Draper et al, 2013).

As least one diversion programme for young offenders has used yoga, meditation, and mindfulness-based interventions as an alternative to imprisonment, on the basis that mindfulness teachings could complement and reinforce other cognitive behavioural interventions (Barret, 2017).

Villeneuve and her colleagues (Villeneuve, F.-Dufour, and Farrall, 2021) argue that it is possible to support desistance by providing practical help and resources based on desisters' needs and providing sustained positive feedback and encouragement to assist in changes in self-identity. Interventions in support of desistance are possible in correctional settings and informal settings. They can help participants acquire or develop potentialities, skills, and resources, which, in turn, foster a positive self-image and the development of prosocial networks, and nurture hope for brighter futures (F.-Dufour, Villeneuve, and Peron, 2018).

Unfortunately, measuring the outcomes of any programme aimed at preventing recidivism and assisting desistance can be quite challenging. Reoffending alone is a poor metric for gauging programme success. Recidivism or re-conviction, for instance, is as much a measure of how people and systems respond to alleged reoffending as it is of behavioural change. It is also a binary measure, and desistance from crime is a complicated process (Klingele, 2019). More nuanced metrics are required.

Implications for programming

Intervention programmes that are embedded within an understanding of the desistance process are urgently needed

(Deuchar et al, 2016: 739). Theoretically, at least, sport-based recidivism prevention programmes can be developed to support or accelerate the desistance process as we currently understand it. Together with other interventions, such as mentoring, cognitive behavioural training, or resettlement assistance, sport-based programmes may help offenders to find their own pathways to desistance.

Building on current knowledge of the desistance process, the programmes should aim to:

- contribute to developing new or existing motivation to change, as well as building new skills, capabilities, and capacities for making different life choices and living differently;
- help youth to build social capital, reconstruct their social identity, and connect with supportive individuals;
- recognize and reinforce efforts to change;
- support positive personal development in a way that relates to gender and cultural differences as well as to different social and cultural contexts;
- help youth to develop hopefulness and a sense of agency and increased control over the direction of their life;
- work with partners, families, friends, and communities to find ways together to support people through desistance;
- help youth to fight the stigmatization that results from their contacts with the justice system;
- offer prosocial modelling in their interactions with youth.

FIVE

Theory of Change Underlying Sport-Based Programmes

As discussed in previous chapters, the relationship between sport and crime has been difficult to disentangle. Some argue that involvement with sport results in a variety of positive impacts for youth including increases in resiliency, self-esteem, self-efficacy, and a wider network of relationships and opportunities (Morgan and Costas Batlle, 2019; Morgan, Parker, and Roberts, 2019; Morgan et al, 2019). Others have noted that there is a link between sport participation and involvement in certain types of delinquency including violence and problematic alcohol use (Stansfield, 2017). It is very clear that involvement in sport can impact different aspects of one's personality and social setting in both positive and negative ways. It is also quite clear that risk-based theories of youth crime prevention rest on shaky evidence and that youth development interventions, through sports or other forms of interventions, must demonstrate how they can produce tangible crime prevention outcomes.

According to a recent UNODC desk review (Samuel, 2018), sport-based crime prevention programmes with well-developed methodologies and robust theories of change are the exception rather than the rule. Most programmes fall into the category of local grassroots initiatives, often established by youth for youth, with limited resources and capacity, with only broad identifiable goals, and with no clearly identifiable methodologies or documented assessments of their effectiveness (Samuel, 2018: 62).

There have been several attempts to develop a theory of positive development through sports (Coalter, 2013a; Noble and Coleman, 2016; Holt et al, 2017) and at least one attempt to propose a theoretical framework that links sports to positive youth development (PYD) and crime prevention (Morgan et al, 2019). Despite substantial research progress in the last decade, there is a lack of a clear and coherent theoretical conception of these sport-based prevention programmes, an understanding of how and why they might be expected to work, and, therefore, how they can most effectively be implemented.

This chapter presents an attempt to conceptualize the links between criminological theory and sport-based crime prevention programmes. This is a prerequisite to forming a cogent theory to explain how sport-based programmes can, at least theoretically, produce crime prevention outcomes at the individual level. This involves clarifying existing concepts and connecting them to existing theories commonly used to understand youth offending and desistance from crime. The focus here is on understanding how participation in sport-based prevention programmes at the community level may affect the likelihood that the targeted youth will become or continue to be involved with criminal activities or criminal groups.

Drift, delinquency, and sport: a starting point

Matza's theory of drift and delinquency explains that youth become involved in crime through a process that involves the slow loosening of social control or what is known as 'drift' (Matza, 1964/1990). Because young people have less of a stake in society and more time for leisure activities, nearly all of them are in a constant state of drift in which criminal activity is a constant temptation. Leisure activities are associated with what Matza called 'subterranean values', which often involve thrill-seeking and masculine displays of aggressiveness. Based on this description it should come as no surprise that there can be considerable overlap between leisure activities and delinquency.

Moffitt (1993) provides some support for the notion that criminal opportunities tend to be ubiquitous for young people. She explains that data from epidemiological studies using the self-report method indicate that almost all adolescents do commit some illegal acts and that studies using official records of arrest by police find surprisingly high prevalence rates.

While it may be true that many juveniles engage in some sort of criminal activity, this does not mean that serious or high levels of youth criminal activity should be considered normal. For example, many adolescents engage in underage drinking, illegal drug use, and minor crime like theft or vandalism; however, more serious types of crime involving violence, persistent criminal activity, and gang involvement are not viewed as normal child development experiences. In an analysis of data from the Cambridge Study in Delinquent Development, Basto-Pereira and colleagues (2020) found that a key research issue in criminology is understanding how and why some people exceed normative levels of offending between the expected beginning in adolescence and the expected end in adulthood. This suggests that it may be important to think in terms of preventing an entrenchment in a criminal career, or perhaps disrupting a criminal career, rather than in terms of absolute desistance from crime.

Given that the vast majority of young people are in a state of drift and are tempted to engage in delinquency on a daily basis and take part in criminal activity at high levels, it seems reasonable to suggest that theories of desistance might offer some insight into their decisions to avoid delinquent activities.[1] Sport is merely one factor that may play a role in criminal involvement (Morgan, Parker, and Roberts, 2019). However, programmes with a solid theoretical basis and a grounding in research could be an effective tool for supporting desistance or disengagement from criminal activities, and reducing the likelihood of persistent criminal involvement.

The model proposed here considers a range of factors and attempts to specify the interrelationships among them (see Figure 5.1 for a graphic depiction of the model). It is important to note at this point that this is not to suggest that mere participation in sports activities can prevent criminal behaviour. Indeed, as noted earlier, it may have the opposite effect by providing more opportunities to get into trouble. Rather, the goal is to specify the conditions and factors that may increase the likelihood of success of sport-based crime prevention programmes. The chapter identifies key concepts derived from various theories based on individual differences and personality development and then attempts to address social-psychological concerns identified by desistance and social support theories.

Psychological and social capital: what makes the difference?

Research has shown that certain life events like getting married and getting a good job can serve as 'hooks for change' in adult offenders (Giordano, Cernkovich, and Rudolph, 2002). In a similar vein, as was seen earlier, it is often suggested that sport can be used as a hook or relationship strategy with which an intervention can be undertaken (Nichols, 2007). Giordano and her colleagues (2002) have identified four aspects of the cognitive transformation that offenders undergo when they decide to desist from crime. First, they must have an openness to change for any event to have an impact. Second, the person must define the event as meaningful and come to the determination that their previous delinquent behaviour is fundamentally incompatible with the new situation. Third, the event must impact the person enough that they begin to see themselves in a new light – they craft a replacement identity. Fourth, the person will begin to reinterpret their past problematic behaviour in a new light. It seems that, in their decision to distance themselves from

Figure 5.1: Participation in sports programmes and crime: development of psychological, human, and social capital

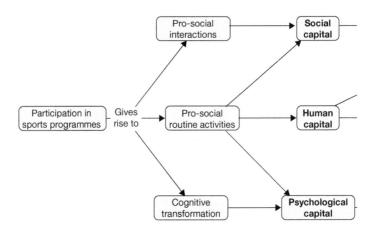

delinquent behaviour, youth might experience a shift like the one described.

Morgan, Parker, and Roberts (2019) contend that through sports, participants often develop psychological capital which can be helpful when accessing opportunities that enhance one's sense of social inclusion (for example, school, employment). Psychological capital consists of four components including self-efficacy, hope, optimism, and resilience. They go on to acknowledge that sport participation may also raise levels of human and social capital in participants but then claim

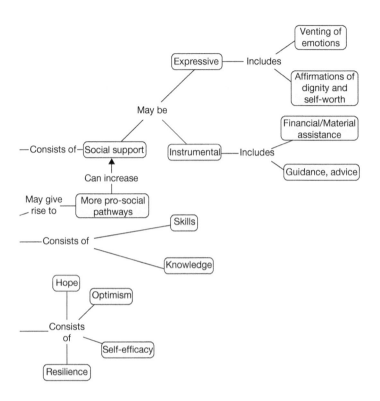

that: 'simple accumulation these forms of capital may, in themselves, be insufficient in acquiring employment, and with it, social inclusion' (Morgan, Parker, and Roberts, 2019: 1102). Despite this caveat, according to some criminological theories of desistance, social capital plays an important role in decisions to distance oneself from crime. For example, Laub and Sampson (2003), based on their extensive research and age-graded theory of informal social control, believe that cognitive transformation is not a requirement for desistance. They had observed that men desisted from crime largely because they were able to capitalize on key structural and situational circumstances. They explained that '[m]any men make a commitment to go straight without even realizing it. Before they know it, they have invested so much in a marriage or a job they did not want to risk losing their investment' (Laub and Sampson, 2003: 278–9).

Given that there's strong evidence that young people tend to be in a state of 'drift' and that delinquent opportunities are ubiquitous for many of them, one could argue that social capital may be of particular importance to reorienting those tempted to engage in crime (Coalter, 2013a). As described earlier, Morgan and his colleagues identified several aspects of psychological capital that might be cultivated through participation in sports programmes (Morgan, Parker, and Roberts, 2019). It is important to note that the current literature does not support the notion that participation in sport alone can enhance these qualities and also to note that not all sports are created equally in terms of their potential to effect positive changes in individuals (Morgan et al, 2020). Morgan and his colleagues also identified human or social capital as a benefit, noting that this is the standard focus in most policy interventions; however, this concept and the processes associated with it are still vague and unspecified (Morgan et al, 2020).

The next section expands on the notion of psychological capital by using Deci and Ryan's self-determination theory (Deci and Ryan, 2000). It also begins to specify various elements of social capital using Cullen's social support theory (Cullen, 1994; Colvin, Cullen, and Vander Ven, 2002).

Expanding on psychological capital and specifying social capital

In their self-determination theory Deci and Ryan offer an interesting avenue for expanding on the concept of psychological capital (Deci and Ryan, 2000). More specifically, they argue that humans have basic psychological needs just as they have physiological needs (for example, food and water). They go on to identify three of these psychological needs: competence, relatedness, and autonomy. *Competence* refers to the innate desire to master skills and knowledge and shares much in common with the concept of self-efficacy. *Relatedness* is the psychological need to feel connected to a group and needed by other people. *Autonomy* focuses on the need to feel like behaviour is freely chosen and congruent with the beliefs of the individual. As will be demonstrated later, these elements are helpful for specifying how psychological capital affects decision-making processes around criminal involvement and desistance from crime.

A great deal of research suggests that social networks are important in the desistance process for adult criminals. In their research, Laub and Sampson (2003) found that habitual offenders who desisted from crime drew heavily upon resources and support from their social networks that developed from personal relationships established in prosocial activities and important life events (for example, getting married, getting a good job, having children):

> Generally, the persistent offenders we interviewed experienced residential instability, marital instability, job instability, failure in school and the military, and relatively long periods of incarceration. ... In contrast to the men who desisted from crime, the life of the persistent offender was marked by marginality and a lack of structure that led to even more situations conducive to crime. For those without permanent addresses, steady jobs, spouses, children and other rooted forms of life, crime and deviance is an unsurprising result – even for those possessing so-called prosocial traits. As a consequence of chaotic and unstructured routines, one has contact with individuals who are similarly situated – in these cases, the similarly unattached and free from nurturing social

capital or support, and informal social control. (Laub and Sampson, 2003: 280)

Obviously, young people have much different concerns from the men Laub and Sampson were studying. However, it is possible that the social networks that can be developed by youth through participation in sport could provide a similarly 'rooted form of life'. Unfortunately, social capital does not have clearly specified or consistent definition in the literature, and this makes it difficult to translate into a variable and measure. Cullen's social support theory (1994) offers some insight into how one might further conceptualize social capital.

The theory of social support identifies two key dimensions of social support: expressive and instrumental (Colvin, Cullen, and Vander Ven, 2002). Examples of *expressive social support* include the venting of emotions and affirmations of dignity and self-worth. *Instrumental social support* refers to not only material and/or financial assistance but also providing advice, guidance, and connections that offer aid and opportunity for advancement in legitimate society. Colvin and colleagues go on to state that: 'social supports reduce the impact of strain by providing resources that allow individual to cope with adversity through non-criminal means' (Colvin, Cullen, and Vander Ven, 2002: 24). The consistency of the social support is key to its effectiveness in reducing crime. Erratic social support does not have the potential to develop the necessary sense of trust between the recipient and giver for a strong social bond to form. Further, it may cause some people to drift and seek alternative support from deviant sources (Colvin, Cullen, and Vander Ven, 2002). Social support that is reliable helps to reduce strain and anger and to generate a stronger internalized sense of self-control that can lead to positive outcomes.

Differential sources of social support are a key dimension to this theory – it is important to consider the source of the support and the possible impact that this could have on the outcome. More specifically, if social support come from illegitimate sources, it may also come with access to an illegitimate opportunity structure that provides 'knowledge, skills, connections, role models, a sense of belonging, and social status that promote success in various criminal activities' (Colvin, 2002: 25) and the development of criminal capital. If illegitimate social support is blocked, the person may resort to more unskilled and disorganized forms of delinquency.

Cross-level theory of change for sport and crime

The factors identified thus far can also help inform the logic behind the theory of change associated with sports programmes that focus on crime prevention. For Coalter (2013) and Morgan and his colleagues (2019), an intelligent crime prevention policy must acknowledge 'the necessity to shift the perspective through which the theory of change is developed away from families of programmes (such as those related to sport and crime desistance) towards families of mechanisms which capture the 'processes, relationships and experiences that might achieve the desired [programme] outcomes' (Coalter, 2013a: 607), in this case desistance from crime.

There are two general steps involved with articulating a theory of change. First, one must state the change or transformation that the programme hopes to obtain. In the case of sport-based crime prevention programmes, this would be prevention of criminal behaviour for those not involved in such behaviour, and desistance or disengagement from persistent youth crime[2] for those who have had problems in the past. Second, it is important to clearly articulate the assumptions and logical steps that give rise to the desired outcome (Fox, Grimm, and Caldeira, 2017).

Morgan and his colleagues (2020) identified three phases involved with developing a theory of change that explains how sport-based programmes encourage desistance from crime. *Phase One* describes the initial engagement with the programme and the key 'hook characteristics'. These include: choosing an activity that is popular and interesting to youth; allowing youth to feel a sense of control or ownership over the activity; making the activity accessible to youth; providing an activity that is a release or distraction for the participants while still being culturally relevant; and ensuring the activity is conducted in a safe and neutral space. While all of these are important considerations, it seems that some are obvious (for example, making sure the activity is popular among target audience and is conducted in a non-threatening environment). Building on ideas from Cullen's theory of social support, one could argue that consistency should also be considered a key component to initial engagement. Activities should be regularly held and there should be a clear schedule of when they take place or when they can be accessed.

Consistency is also important when considering *Phase Two* of Morgan and his associates' theory of change – this phase consists of three components (Morgan et al, 2020). First, they mention that it is crucial to construct trusting relationships within the programme; it is difficult to trust a source that is inconsistent and erratic. Second, it is also important to enable the participants to feel valued and that their abilities are recognized. Interestingly, this is key element of expressive social support as described by Cullen (1994). Third, coaches and programme leaders must be role models and have a nuanced understanding of the local culture and community issues.

Based on the tenets of the self-determination theory paradigm, one can specify the conditions that ought to be present for these processes to occur. For example, to support competence, programmes ought to provide clear rules and expectations of behaviour, should offer opportunities to develop skills, present challenges that are achievable, and feedback that is constructive and positive (Petrich, 2020). Further, according to Petrich, 'support for relatedness is optimized when an individual experiences acknowledgement, care, and genuine interest from others, as well as where relationships are experienced as cooperative' (Petrich, 2020: 356). Lastly, autonomy can be fostered through efforts to understand the perspectives of the participants, supporting choices, using non-coercive measures, and providing meaningful explanations for changes and consequences. Conditions that can thwart the fulfilment of psychological needs include use of punishments and rewards, surveillance, evaluations, use of coercive language or action to control behaviour, feeling rejected or shamed by the group, and being made to feel incompetent (Morgan et al, 2019b).

In *Phase Three* intermediate outcomes of the intervention are considered. More specifically, it is thought that participants can increase levels of psychological and human capital through activities occurring in the first two phases of the project. In this theory of change, human capital bears very little resemblance to the notion of social capital or social support described earlier, as Morgan and his colleagues (2020) focus almost exclusively on how relationships lead to educational and employment opportunities. While this is clearly an important aspect of instrumental social support, the benefits of mentorship, advice, and guidance gained from these relationships and the impact this has on identity, personality, and psychological capital may have been overlooked.

A problem with other theories in this area is that they fail to identify the causal mechanism(s) that lead to prevention of criminality and desistance in young people. They seem to assume that if a young person's psychological, social, and human capital can be slightly increased a miracle will occur, and they will avoid or disengage from criminal behaviour. However, a substantial number of criminals are quite self-confident, resilient, and socially connected, and possess a variety of skills that could help them succeed in life, and yet they still choose to participate in crime anyway. The key is to explain how having these forms of capital impacts the immediate decision-making process and also various factors associated with criminal behaviour.

One can argue that human, social, and psychological capital have an impact on the cost-benefit analysis that is commonly employed by young people who are in a state of drift – they have more to lose in terms of participation in the activity and relationships tied to the activity than a person not involved. Further, criminal and deviant behaviour become less attractive because they already have activities that provide a change of pace and involve elements of thrill-seeking and risk-taking. The 'sneaky thrills' associated with some types of crime (for example, theft, drug use, drug dealing) and the positive labelling that makes these acts enticing are important factors that are often ignored or downplayed by criminologists, who tend to focus on psychological, social, and economic factors (Katz, 1988; Brezina and Aragones, 2004).

Sports programmes may be helpful in cultivating the basic psychological needs identified by Deci and Ryan's self-determination theory and can offer insights into how the decision-making process may be affected in this case. One must consider that, in some cases, youth fill these needs through criminal activity, and a young person might derive a feeling of accomplishment from being a particularly lucrative drug dealer, being able to produce high-quality meth, or having the necessary skills to steal expensive cars. The social connections made through criminal ventures or as part of a gang or organized crime group can provide a sense of relatedness. The freedom from work and school that accompanies a criminal lifestyle can also provide a sense of autonomy. The various forms of capital that result from participation in sport can provide competition with these criminal opportunities and can alter the cost-benefit analysis that many young people consider before partaking in delinquency.

The spoils of human, social, and psychological capital can also impact motivational factors that often pull people towards criminal activities. First, the development of these forms of capital changes how young people deal with strain in their lives – they have more social support, more people to talk to for advice, and a greater inner reserve to draw from when dealing with adverse or noxious situations. Second, the influence of delinquent peers and acquaintances is less pronounced because the young people have other relationships made through sport that are built on a non-deviant foundation – this may also serve to break ties with delinquent groups that may have been present previously. Third, the hook provided by involvement with sports programmes and the relationships that develop can impact the attachments and connections to outside social institutions associated with the activity (for example, school, religious, or youth organizations and clubs).

The discussion around the role of life-skills development begs the question: How are these skills most effectively translated from sports to school, work, and family life? As Armour and Sanford suggest, a simplistic conception of skills transfer may obscure the process:

> Certainly the data and the wider Positive Youth Development (PYD) literature provide evidence to suggest that, at the very least, specific planning for skill transfer should be built into project design. Yet, it is also possible to question the validity of the whole notion of 'transfer' in the context of learning. (Armour and Sandford, 2013: 102)

As previously discussed, more effort needs to be devoted to understanding how skills developed in sports programmes are used in other areas of life and the processes that encourage this activity. Gould and Carson (2008) attempt to further specify important factors based on the research while also warning about negative impacts of sports programmes:

> These findings and others focusing on different life skills have led researchers to conclude that sport has the potential to facilitate life skills development in young people. However, this growth does not occur from merely participating in programs. Life skills must be specifically targeted and taught in environments that are conducive

for doing so (for example, supportive coaches, clear rules and responsibilities, and positive social norms. (…) It is also important to note that negative social–emotional growth and inappropriate attitudes and behaviours may be developed if sport is not conducted in the right manner. (Gould and Carson, 2008: 63)

Several other studies have also found that skills obtained through or developed in sports programmes need to be cultivated if they are to be applied to other life domains (Armour and Sandford, 2013; Allen and Rhind, 2019).

The theory of change proposed here differs from that of Morgan and his associates (Morgan et al, 2020) in several respects (see Figure 5.2 for a graphic depiction). First, the notion of cognitive transformation, from Giordano and colleagues, has been used to further elaborate on the process

Figure 5.2: Alliance of sport theory of change

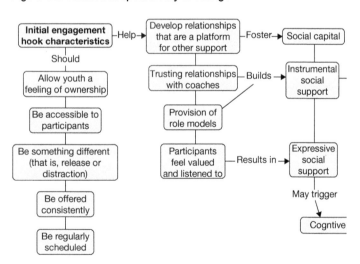

Source: Adapted from Morgan, Parker, Meek, and Cryer (2019)

behind the accumulation of psychological capital. Second, an important aspect of programme engagement has been identified and the general importance of maintaining consistent and regularly scheduled activities was noted. Third, based on Laub and Sampson's well-supported theory of desistance, the importance of social capital beyond its impact on employment and educational opportunities was seriously considered. More specifically, we contend that the networks that come along with high levels of social capital may impact one's levels of psychological capital and offer important expressive social support for at-risk youth. Fourth, the meaning of social capital is more fully specified by using Cullen's theory of social support as an elaborative device.

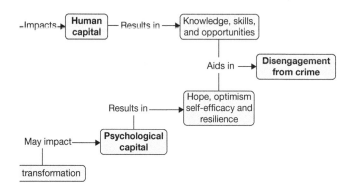

SIX

Emerging Good Practices

This chapter identifies some emerging good practices in youth crime prevention through sports. This is based on both a review of the relevant research and also discussions and interviews with coaches and leaders of sport-based crime prevention programmes in British Columbia. Based on these interviews, the findings of recent research and the conclusions of the UN Expert Group meeting referred to earlier (United Nations, 2020), a consensus is emerging around programme practices and characteristics that are most likely to yield substantial positive youth development (PYD) outcomes and encourage the development of valuable social, human, and psychological capital for participants. Until rigorous programme evaluations can provide more specific programme development guidance, the goal should be to maximize the value and potential impact of crime prevention interventions through sports.

Notwithstanding the fact that the crime prevention outcomes associated with these programmes have yet to be more conclusively demonstrated, it would be wise to let the development of sport-based crime prevention programmes be guided by several evidence-based principles. First among them is the idea that the programme's rationale or logical framework should be clearly specified and related tightly to crime prevention goals. The programme should also: be context specific, culturally relevant, gender responsive and responsive to the specific needs of the targeted group; rely on effective and non-discriminatory recruitment strategies; remain mindful of the need to ensure a safe environment; and avoid further stigmatizing vulnerable or marginalized youth. Other principles concerning effective programme delivery should be considered, including engaging parents and family members, and strengthening the role of positive peer influence as well as the role of facilitators and coaches. Each of these principles are reviewed briefly in this chapter.

Well-articulated crime prevention objectives and programme rationale

The specific crime prevention objectives of a sport-based programme must be explicit and articulated based on a clear and credible theory of change. The programme rationale or logical framework should specify what in the chosen sports activities and accompanying interventions can be logically expected to lead to crime prevention outcomes.

The programme should be grounded in a strength-based approach aimed at enhancing protective factors and mitigating risk factors. It should provide youth with opportunities for learning, personal growth, success, and recognition, and offer expressive social support (for example, affirmations of worth and dignity of participants, a sympathetic ear, advice) (Cameron and MacDougall, 2000; Catalano et al, 2002; Coalter, 2013a; Armour, Sandford, and Duncombe, 2013; Roth and Brooks-Gunn, 2016).

Research has shown that PYD is not necessarily achieved through mere participation in sports. Sport-based programmes are most likely to be successful as crime prevention initiatives when combined with strategies or mentoring that address issues of social and personal development. Programmes must be intentionally structured to achieve their PYD goals. *Intentionality* refers to programme designs that deliberately and strategically create opportunities that maximize developmental outcomes, in particular by fostering life skills development and life skills transfer. The intervention should be *deliberately structured* to teach life skills and help youth develop core competencies. Intentionally structured programmes score higher on programme quality and PYD outcomes than non-intentionally structured programmes (Turnnidge, Côté, and Hancock, 2014).

The acquisition of life skills is unlikely to be sufficient to prevent crime. There are many criminals – career criminals and even dangerous criminals – with excellent life skills which they know how to put to good criminal use. A specific kind of intentionality is probably necessary to link skills development to crime prevention: an intentional crime prevention approach is necessary. It is essential that this second level of intentionality focuses on targeting changes in values, attitudes, motivation, and adhesion to a culture of respect for others and lawfulness, and all this is obviously related to identity.

Context-specific programming

Sports programmes should be evidence-based and tailored to the local context, interests, and cultural background of the young people they seek to influence. They must address the local crime situation and respond to local crime prevention goals and priorities. Programmes should also adopt a flexible approach capable of responding to changes in the local context and the challenges that inevitably arise during programme implementation. Because interventions that produced crime prevention outcomes in a certain context cannot be assumed to be immediately transferrable to all contexts, models applied in a new context must be adapted or developed locally. Decentralized programmes and participatory approaches to programme design involve intended beneficiaries and their community in the planning process and take local needs and assets into consideration. It is essential to consider how the design, location, and funding of sporting and recreational infrastructure contributes to social cohesion and avoids taking sport and physical activity out of its social context (Cameron and MacDougall, 2000).

Responsiveness to the needs of the targeted youth

Programmes must align their objectives with the youth's specific needs (Nichols, 1997; Cameron and MacDougall, 2000; Crabbe, 2000; Sandford, Duncombe, and Armour, 2008; Ehsani, Dehnavi, and Heidary, 2012; Armour and Sandford, 2013; Chamberlain, 2013; Armour, Sandford, and Duncombe, 2013; Fagan and Lindsey, 2014; Mason, Cleland, and Aldridge, 2017; Bailey, 2018). Sport-based interventions must be sensitive to the diverse needs of young people, particularly if they are to tackle the underlying structural inequalities that are arguably responsible for youth crime (Chamberlain, 2013). It has been suggested that, given the magnitude of personality differences among programme participants, practitioners involved in sport-based or other PYD programmes would benefit from policies and programme designs which incorporate personality assessment of the participants (Anderson, 2017).

Needs support may play a significant role in facilitating psychosocial outcomes for youth. It is important to deliver high-quality programmes that support basic psychological needs and foster psychosocial development in youth. Research has emphasized the value of structuring youth sport programmes to satisfy basic needs, which may have positive implications on youth mental health (Bean, Kendellen, and Forneris, 2016a; Bean and Forneris, 2019; Bean et al, 2020, 2021).

Gender responsiveness

There is a need for a wide range of safe and accessible sport-based programmes for young women and girls, programmes that are gender-responsive and respectful of cultural differences. In truth, however, the absence of clear etiological information regarding the risk and protective factors that are most influential for males and females in a particular context makes 'gender-responsive' prevention programming difficult, given the goal is to ensure that interventions address the risks, needs, and protective factors that are most salient for each gender group (Fagan and Lindsey, 2014).

The development of programmes that are responsive to the special needs and interests of girls and young women can be facilitated by: consulting with women and girls during programme design, implementation, and evaluation; drawing on existing expertise from organizations already involved in promoting the participation of women and girls in sport; applying safeguards and trauma-informed strategies and practices for women and girls in sport-based interventions; ensuring that interventions address the risk and protective factors that are most salient for each gender group; recruiting female coaches and facilitators; and developing capacity among facilitators, coaches, trainers, and sports leaders both to act as positive role models and to challenge gender stereotypes, norms, and attitudes that condone or justify gender-based discrimination and violence (United Nations, 2020).

Cultural relevance of interventions

Socializing experiences that foster positive development and the acquisition of core skills and competencies vary across cultural contexts. Prevention programmes based on skills and competencies development must be culturally relevant.

On the issue of whether participants should be matched with staff based on gender, race, or ethnicity, a recent study by Riciputi and her colleagues (2020) offers a qualified answer. According to the study, the similarity of staff to youth in regard to race and gender impacts the way engagement with programme participant is realized. However, the effect of staff support on emotional engagement was enhanced for youth dissimilar in race/ethnicity to their leader.

Matches between youth and their staff leader on both gender and race/ethnicity directly predicted behavioural engagement, whereas the effect of staff support on emotional engagement was enhanced for youth dissimilar in race/ethnicity to their leader. Staff support may promote engagement in PYD programs, with the similarity of staff to youth on race and gender impacting the manner in which engagement is realized. This study demonstrates the importance of teaching staff the value of interactions with youth from different backgrounds and genders to promote engagement in the programs and support PYD outcomes for all youth. (Riciputi et al, 2020: 55)

There is obviously also a need to better understand youth sport and physical activity from diverse cultural perspectives, particularly the perspectives of Indigenous youth (McHugh et al, 2015; Bruner et al, 2016; Strachan, McHugh, and Mason, 2018). In Canada, for example, there are often obstacles to sport participation among Indigenous youth. Such barriers can result in negative sport and recreation experiences for this group (Bruner et al, 2016). However, sports and recreational activities can create spaces for the positive development of Indigenous youth when these spaces promote holistic health, traditional culture and values, connections to the land, and relationships to Indigenous communities (McHugh et al, 2019; Coppola, Holt and McHugh, 2020). For instance, 'offering sport opportunities that provide connection to the land seems to be a key component for enhancing sport experiences for Indigenous youth' (Strachan, McHugh and Mason, 2018: 299).

Engagement of vulnerable groups, youth safety and non-stigmatization

Vulnerable groups are not homogeneous, and each group presents different challenges that must be considered during the planning and delivery of crime prevention intervention (Fernández-Gavira et al, 2017). The model of intervention must be adapted to the characteristics and circumstances of the group. Very importantly, the participation of youth from vulnerable or at-risk groups should be encouraged without further stigmatizing them.

When working with gang-involved youth, the role of group dynamics in helping youth develop a positive identity is particularly important and should be carefully considered in delivering sport-based interventions. The management of group processes is an important aspect of the role of coaches and facilitators. Understanding group dynamics and interpersonal influence in sport and in the youth's environment is important because the group environment is a fundamental determinant of individual outcomes such as performance, interpersonal development, and motivation (Evans et al, 2013). Programmes should remain mindful of the substantial positive impact of cooperative goal structures on early adolescents' achievement and peer relationships across numerous domains. The management of group processes is an important concern for coaches and practitioners.

Youth must be able to participate in sports and physical activities in settings where they feel physically safe; personally valued; morally, and economically supported; personally empowered; and hopeful about their future. Providing a safe and supportive environment is an essential prerequisite to successful sport-based crime prevention programmes. A successful intervention requires an environment in which youth feel physically and emotionally comfortable and safe (Eccles, Gootman, and Appleton, 2002; Morris et al, 2004). The experiences and opportunities that sport provides are not different from other life situations, and, therefore, it is reasonable to assume that a positive environment is the best way to promote youth development through sport participation (Côté and Hancock, 2016).

Effective recruitment strategies

For sports to act as a credible mechanism through which crime might be reduced or prevented, an important first step is to engage and retain the target population with the sport-based activity (Vandermeerschen, Vos, and Scheerder, 2013; Morgan and Costas Batlle, 2019), while minimizing the risk of them becoming labelled as 'problem youth'.

For the sport to act as a 'hook', the sports activity must be popular among the target group, and the youth must possess a clear sense of ownership and control over the activities that are offered and delivered through an intervention (Crabbe et al, 2006; Coalter, 2007). A programme's recruitment strategy can obviously have a direct impact on its outcomes. Programmes must have an effective, non-discriminatory, and non-stigmatizing youth recruitment strategy aligned with the programme objectives and a clear definition of the intended programme beneficiaries. Attracting and retaining hard-to-reach youth is difficult. Involving such youth requires most programmes to strengthen their outreach, recruitment, and programming strategies (Zeldin, 2004).

Recruitment assumes greater importance within sport-based programmes that promote social inclusion and are 'aimed at development among otherwise marginalized, disaffected youth who can be difficult to locate much less engage' (Hartmann and Kwauk, 2011: 290). It is advisable to decouple recruitment in the programme from an individual risk assessment and to reach out to youth without risking their further stigmatization.

In practice, many programmes have diffuse ideas of a 'target group', usually some 'at-risk' youth group (Coalter, 2013a). This was certainly the case of most of the programmes reviewed in British Columbia. As a result, programme managers often have difficulty ensuring that the target population is engaged with the programme (or the right programme, relevant to the youth's needs and circumstances) and stays engaged with it. Youth who may have the most to gain from a sport-based programme do not necessarily volunteer to participate.

Some programmes use recruitment strategies which tend to exclude certain youth in need of support or intervention. For example, following the competitive sport logic, many sport-based programmes continue to use performance-based or experience-based criteria for recruiting youth, using try-outs for the youth to qualify or past experience/training in a given sport. The competitive nature of the recruitment process results in some youth not 'making the grade', failing the try-outs, being excluded from participating. This only reinforces the experience of many adolescents who may feel ostracized and disillusioned and may turn to less healthy or socially acceptable activities to compensate, find solace, or feel accepted.

Other programmes recruit youth based on a police referral to the programme, the youth's place of residence, or some specific sociocultural criteria. These criteria do not necessarily coincide with the objective of reaching youth most in need of the intervention. It is usually insufficient also to rely on sports clubs and volunteers for recruiting youth into programmes that are relevant to their needs and circumstances (Morgan and Costas Batlle, 2019).

Jacobs, Wahl-Alexander, and Mack (2019) have identified several best practices for gaining access to non-traditional, hard-to-access environments. They suggested that careful planning and persistence is needed to protect youth and provide a safe environment, choose appropriate sport content, identify realistic positive outcomes, foster buy-in from partners, and design a programme customized to youths' wants and needs.

However, disadvantaged contexts can also pose problems for obtaining a consistent stream of resources and can incorporate tensions from the streets, such as territorial battles between gangs, into intervention activities. Sport-based interventions can also have a negative impact on youth violence, and this has been reported in cases of young people being referred to programmes by the police, young offenders' institutions, and schools (McMahon and Belur, 2013). An awareness of the possibility of violence can aid programmes to plan against it.

Sustained interventions

Programmes should offer intensive and lasting interventions through sustained delivery mechanisms that engage youth in the long term and enable lasting relationships (Mason, Cleland, and Aldridge, 2017). More effective programmes tend to build a structure to ensure sustainability. They consistently involve youth for a longer period (at least nine months), are well supervised, and include some sustained parental involvement (Mahoney and Stattin, 2000; Catalano et al, 2002; Caldwell and Smith, 2006; Armour and Sandford, 2013; Mason, Cleland, and Aldridge, 2017; Berdychevsky, Stodolska, and Shinew, 2022). Programmes should encourage a gradual take-up of responsibilities, thereby increasing the youth's engagement at their own pace (Buelens et al, 2017).

Programme retention is also crucial to achieving positive development and crime prevention outcomes. Duration and continuity of participation in the programme have been shown to positively correlate with participants' developmental assets such as relationships, values, skills, abilities, and a positive self-perception developed over time (Reverdito et al, 2017).

In one study, participants in a sport-based PYD programme designed to engage youth through running completed a post programme survey measuring their self-determined motivation towards running and achievement of developmental outcomes. Participants with higher self-determined motivation towards running reported higher general self-efficacy, more positive attitudes towards a healthy lifestyle, and lower engagement in threatening behaviour (Inoue et al, 2015).

Programme retention and the factors associated with youth decisions to opt out or drop out of sport-based programmes need further examination. It appears that processes both external and internal to the sports activity or the programme sometimes work together in ways that amplify feelings of not belonging in the programme (Persson et al, 2019). As previously mentioned, the experience of bullying, abuse, and violence may also drive some youth away from a programme they had enthusiastically participated in. Unfortunately, very few programmes collect data on participants who opt out of the programme and the factors associated with that decision. It may be that the very factors (including social and developmental factors) that put these youth at risk in the first place are also responsible for the same youth dropping out.

A well-planned delivery

Eccles, Gootman, and Appleton identified the programme-setting features of effective positive development programmes: (1) physical and psychological safety; (2) appropriate structure; (3) supportive relationships; (4) opportunities to belong; (5) positive social norms; (6) support for efficacy and mattering; (7) opportunities for skill building; and (8) integration of family, school, and community efforts (Eccles, al Gootman, and Appleton, 2002).

Programmes must recognize the significance of social relationships, create a sense of community, employ a multi-agency approach, build a structure to ensure sustainability, and incorporate credible monitoring and evaluation (Sandford, Armour, and Duncombe, 2007). A flexible approach is also necessary to allow programme activities to respond to changes in the local context and to challenges that inevitably arise (Mason, Cleland, and Aldridge, 2017).

Programme activities should be attractive and preferably take place outside the school to reach out to youth for whom school engagement is problematic (Astbury, Knight, and Nichols, 2005; Armour, Sandford, and Duncombe, 2013; Berdychevsky, Stodolska, and Shinew, 2022). Part of the attraction of sport-based programmes is that the activities through which they are delivered involve a much-respected and sought-after level of skill and ability. Youth are more likely to engage with a programme if it teaches them something they think is worth knowing (Crabbe, 2000). The sports activities included in the programme should be respond to the interests of the youth targeted by the programme. The programme should probably downplay the competitive elements of sports activities (Morris et al, 2004) and emphasize internal motivation and individualized standards of success in a task-oriented setting.

Competitive sports reflect the social environment in which vulnerable youth have already experienced hardship, exclusion, and failure. In that regard, they can have a negative effect. Additionally, bullying in sports settings is perceived to be more likely to occur in unstructured competitive environments with limited supervision.

For some youth, it is important to de-emphasise the achievement of socially defined standards of success:

> The research has demonstrated that, for some children, the activity must de-emphasise the achievement of societally defined standards in a competitive setting. Since many of these children already know that by society's standards they are 'losers,' they do not need to be reminded of this in their play activity. For the most sensitive children, sport activity should be either individual or small group in structure, in which minimal amounts of co-operative behaviour are expected. It should possess an element of thrill and excitement as delinquent youths have a tendency to depress the magnitude of environmental stimuli with the result that they often need greater amounts of stimulation in order to become motivated. (Andrews and Andrews, 2003: 547)

Views about the purpose and place of competition within youth sports remain polarized (Camiré, 2015). There are also questions about whether competition is developmentally appropriate and advantageous for youth. Some experts oppose youth participation in competition during the formative developmental stage. It is therefore important to understand the conditions under which youth can grow through competition (Kochanek et al, 2019). Programmes should consider whether the targeted participants for the programme have the required competitive experience and readiness to function in the programme's competitive sports activities.

Interagency cooperation and partnerships

Whenever possible, programmes should aim to integrate family, school, and community efforts to support youth. Programmes can benefit from an interagency cooperation approach, including schools, sports organizations, crime prevention specialists, and, when relevant, the police and criminal justice agencies (Cameron and MacDougall, 2000). Like other types of crime prevention initiatives, sport-based crime prevention programmes are greatly facilitated by coordination and partnerships between different sectors, levels of government, and community organizations. Collaboration with other agencies can broaden the activities the programme offers.

For example, a cooperative relationship between schools and community sports groups can ensure that community-based programmes contribute to school engagement (Morgan and Bush, 2016). A programme's contribution to the development of social and cultural capital is closely associated with its ability to link up with various institutional agents and the provision of a facilitating context for the youth to broaden their social experience (Spaaij, 2012). Similarly, programmes can learn from each other and should be eager to share good practices, tools, and resources with each other.

A review of 12 PYD programmes showed that their implementation varied and was influenced by its context (Dickson et al, 2018). Formal and informal community engagement was a 'key factor in ensuring programmes were culturally sensitive, accessible, and appealing to young people and their parents as well as the wider community' (Dickson et al, 2018: 1118).

Finally, the long-term effectiveness of sport-based crime prevention programmes depends on whether they are combined with critically informed strategies to alter the social and economic factors that are responsible for risk of criminal involvement and victimization. Sport-based crime prevention programmes must be sensitive to the diverse needs and circumstances of vulnerable youth if they are to tackle the underlying structural inequalities that are partly responsible for youth crime. To that end, an inclusive approach to partnership development is essential to the long-term success of any 'bottom-up' approach to promoting sport-based interventions as a crime prevention and rehabilitation tool (Chamberlain, 2013: 1289).

Engaged parents, family members, and other significant adults

Social interactions in the educational context created by a sport-based programmes are central to how individuals learn life skills and develop core competencies. Interactions with peers, parents, and coaches are crucial components of how people learn life skills through their involvement in sport (Holt and Tamminen, 2009).

Quality interactions between the youth and key social agents (peers, parents, teachers, and coaches) and the integration of family, school and community efforts are important for the success of sport-based prevention programmes. Families are a crucial part of sport participation and skills development. Family members and contexts play an active role in the acquisition and application of life skills (Hodge et al, 2017). Parents who are aware of their child's leisure interests, activities, and friends are a protective factor (Caldwell and Smith, 2006). Programmes should therefore find practical ways to promote meaningful interactions between youth and interested and caring adults, fostering a sense of acceptance and belonging, placing value on individual achievement, encouraging a positive attitude to the future, and helping youth develop an ability to work with others and work out conflicts.

Parents are a critical sport socialization agent for children and adolescents as they are invested emotionally, socially, and monetarily (Dorsch, Smith, and McDonough, 2009; Johansen and Green, 2019; Sutcliffe et al, 2020). For example, a study of a soccer programme showed that the parental praise and understanding, directive behaviour, and pressure were positively related to players' perceived life skills development within soccer (Mossman and Cronin, 2019). Parental engagement in a sport-based programme can have many benefits from the point of view of promoting youth development. However, greater parental involvement does not necessarily coincide with more positive experiences for children, or for the parents (Dorsch, Smith, and McDonough, 2009; Sutcliffe et al, 2020).

Regrettably, the parents' side-line behaviour does not always align with their stated goals for their children's involvement in sport (Dorsch, Smith, and McDonough et al, 2009; Dorsch, Smith, Wilson et al, 2015). In one survey of 107 youth involved in sports as children, 9 out of 10 respondents reported encountering some form of emotionally abusive or intimidating behaviour on the part of other parents (McPherson et al, 2017). Parental antisocial behaviour within the context of the youth participation in sports and its impact on youth can be an issue. There is also the question of whether parents, coaches, and bystanders are willing and prepared to intervene when they witness the antisocial behaviours of certain parents.

The role of parental involvement within the intentional process of psychosocial development through sports requires more attention. Researchers have tried to identify the factors associated with optimal parental involvement that produce PYD outcomes (Harwood et al, 2019). It appears that positive psychosocial outcomes are associated with parental supportive behaviours displayed at home, in training, and at competitions, while negative or detrimental psychosocial outcomes are associated with pressure, particularly in relation to competitions (Knight, Berrow, and Harwood, 2017). Parents need to understand their role and utilize a range of intrapersonal, interpersonal, and organizational skills to support their child, manage themselves, and manage their interactions with others in the youth sport environment (Harwood and Knight, 2015). Programmes can optimize the role of parents by raising their awareness and facilitating opportunities for them to support psychosocial development and collaboration with coaches or improving coach education to facilitate parent–coach relationships (Harwood et al, 2019).

Dorsch, Smith, and McDonough (2015) described a process of socialization of parents through organized sports, through which parents became behaviourally and emotionally engaged in youth sport, began to use sport as a vehicle to teach their children life lessons, and assimilated what was expected of parents into their behaviours in the organized youth sport setting. Through repeated social interactions, parents embraced their emerging roles and became reflective about their development as parents in the context of organized youth sport (Dorsch, Smith, and McDonough, 2015). Interventions that target parents who do not participate in sport may also increase children's participation (Larocca, Wilson, and Cavaliere, 2018).

Lastly, a connection between parents and coaches appears to be important to facilitate psychosocial development and this often depends on the approach or philosophy adopted by coaches and organizations. However, Harwood and his colleagues observed that coaches are the 'gatekeepers' to a child-athlete development programme and are not necessarily supportive of parental engagement (Harwood et al, 2019). This attitude is reflected in the coaches' frequent view of parents as pushy, demanding, overinvolved, or poorly behaved (Knight and Newport, 2017).

Positive peer experiences

Coaches and parents may play important roles in facilitating positive development through a sports programme, but the youth's peers may be even more powerful influencers (Camiré, 2015; Curran and Wexler, 2017). Peer interactions appeared to be a most meaningful aspect of youth sport participation (Holt and Tamminen, 2009). Even when the teaching of life skills is not emphasized in a programme, youth and their peers can produce experiences that support the development of some life skills (Holt et al, 2008).

The right coaches and facilitators

An essential ingredient in youth development through sports is the positive relationships formed with caring adult mentors (that is, coaches, facilitators, support workers) within a carefully structured programme. PYD in sport is more likely when youth have enjoyable and positive immediate experiences in sport (Vierimaa et al, 2017). Coaches who adopt a PYD approach define the desired outcomes of youth sport participation not only in terms of higher levels of participation (engagement) and performance (sport expertise), but also enhanced personal development (for example, life skills, core competencies, and various psychosocial outcomes). These coaches must also be prepared to assume a role as facilitators/catalysts of social inclusion and integration in their capacity as role-models (Eckholm, 2019). Some studies have suggested that coaches who maintain good relationships with their athletes and expose them to 'relatively high levels of sociomoral reasoning within the immediate context of sporting activities' can promote prosocial behaviour (Rutten et al, 2007: 255).

To a very large extent, a sport-based programme is successful only if it recruits and retains qualified trainers, coaches, and facilitators. The coach–participant relationship and the coaches' pedagogical role are central to producing the programme's desired outcomes (Crabbe, 2007; Steinfeldt et al, 2011; Cowan et al, 2012; Taylor, McEwan, and Baker, 2012; Debognies et al, 2019). In sport-based PYD programmes, coaches are expected not only to develop the participants' sport-specific skills, but also to influence other areas of their lives. Mentoring is also seen as an important part of that role (Curran and Wexler, 2017). Therefore, a key aspect of planning and delivering sport-based youth development programmes is the recruitment and training of the individuals who deliver these programmes, especially coaches (Petitpas et al, 2005).

Conflicts are almost unavoidable in a sport context. Sport-based programmes for children and youth offer opportunities for coaches and other adults to teach personal and social responsibility (Jacobs, Wahl-Alexander, and Mack, 2019), but also to help youth learn how to prevent and resolve conflict (Hemphill et al, 2018). Chapter 7 discusses the role of coaches and the strategies they employ, as well as the need for coach training programmes.

SEVEN

Role of Coaches, Mentors, and Facilitators

The coach–athlete relationship is at the heart of coaching (Jowett, 2017) and is central to determining the effects of youth sport participation. Coaches and other programme facilitators have unique opportunities to influence the youth they are working with (Rutten et al, 2007; Côté, Strachan, and Fraser-Thomas, 2008). There may not be a consensus on exactly what differentiates effective from ineffective coaches, but factors such as leadership, expertise, motivation, education, and experience are often cited, together with an ability to form meaningful relationships with youth (Côté and Gilbert, 2009).

Some suggest that coaches must deliberately and systematically integrate life skills development and transfer strategies within their coaching to optimize athlete development (Camiré et al, 2011; Weiss, Bolter, and Kipp, 2014; Bean et al, 2018). The teaching of life skills in sport involves coaches deliberately teaching skills such as goal setting, communication, managing emotions, and developing effective relationships (Camiré and Trudel, 2010). Additionally, coaches involved in programmes for at-risk youth should be sensitive and responsive towards their developmental needs and be reflective of their own behaviour as a role model to maximize the potential of sport-based interventions (Spruit et al, 2018b).

Coaches usually understand the value of life skills integration within sport-based programmes, but they do not always have the knowledge and competencies to explicitly integrate life skills into their coaching practices (Bean and Forneris, 2017). Most youth sport coaches are volunteers who receive little training about youth development through sports (Newman et al, 2018). Training tends to focus on practice design and skill development, rather than on the promotion of positive developmental outcomes. High school sport coaches are typically not equipped with the knowledge, tools, and skills required to deliberately teach life skills (Camiré et al, 2020). Most coaches have little training on how to structure suitable environments to facilitate youth development (Camiré et al, 2011). Although coaches and volunteer staff can coherently describe their coaching practices, they are not particularly interested in theoretical explanations of these practices (Cushion and Partington, 2016).

In British Columbia, for example, coaches involved in community-based sports programmes receive very little training. The training they receive, if any, tends to focus on the technical aspects of coaching, the rules of the game, issues of physical safety and potential liabilities, and sometimes awareness raising around issues such as sexual harassment or other inappropriate behaviour. With one exception, none of the coaches consulted during this review had received training on how to facilitate youth development or on working with vulnerable groups. The exception was a coach who had received some relevant training while studying for a university degree in kinesiology.

Bean, Kramers, Forneris, and Camiré have articulated an empirically-based implicit/explicit continuum of life skills development and transfer distributed across six levels: (a) structuring the sport context; (b) facilitating a positive climate; (c) discussing life skills; (d) practising life skills; (e) discussing transfer; and (f) practising transfer. They observed that life skills development and transfer are optimized (and athletes/participants have a greater likelihood of experiencing positive development outcomes) as coaches move up the continuum (Bean et al, 2018).

A study by Bean and Forneris (2017) revealed that many coaches take on an implicit (as opposed to explicit) approach to teaching life skills, whereby life skills development and transfer are seen as by-products of sport participation. The coaches surveyed for this study refer to the challenges involved in trying to integrate life skills training in coaching activities. They lacked training on how to integrate life skills into their coaching practices (Bean and Forneris, 2017).

Several studies, often based on interviews with successful coaches, have tried to understand the strategies and role of coaches in positive youth development (PYD) and the strategies they utilize (Gould and Carson, 2008; Collins et al, 2009; Flett et al, 2013; Bean and Forneris, 2017). For example, a study of coaches' perceptions revealed four themes: (a) life skills are a by-product of sport participation, and transfer 'just happens'; (b) if intentionally addressed, transfer is reactive (the coach responds to a situation rather than creates the situation); (c) coaches recognize the value of intentionally teaching life skills; and (d) coaches identify challenges associated with using an explicit approach to teaching life skills (Bean and Forneris, 2017).

Flett, Gould, Griffes and Lauer (2013) examined the actions and perceptions of coaches considered to be either more or less effective in terms of their ability to develop the psychosocial skills of youth in underserved settings. They listed some of the characteristics that distinguished more effective from less effective coaches:

- More effective coaches advocate for stronger peer leadership and autonomy in the youth, while less effective coaches try to create a sense of family within the team, but use very negative, militaristic coaching strategies that are not developmentally appropriate.
- More effective coaches tend to prefer strategies that are supportive while challenging players to improve, attempting to develop close relationships along with a positive team climate, and to promote autonomy.

- More effective coaches recognize and prioritize the transfer of psychosocial development beyond sport settings and the transfer of life skills from sport to life, while less effective coaches lack an understanding or specific strategies for transferring lessons learned in sport into non-sport settings.
- More effective coaches appear to be more open to coach training and different ideas (Flett et al, 2013).

Similarly, based on a study of high school football coaches recognized for their abilities to teach life skills, Gould and Carson (2008) identified four sets of factors that were common to the narratives expressed by the coaches:

> First, while highly motivated to win, these coaches had well-developed coaching philosophies that placed prime importance on developing life skills in their players. Second, they had the ability to form strong relationships and to connect with their players. Third, the coaches reported a variety of well-thought-out strategies for teaching the life skills they deemed important. Finally, the respondents recognized that environmental factors (e.g., socioeconomic status) and other individuals (e.g., parents) influenced life skills development and took steps to adapt to, deal with and/or resolve these issues. (Gould and Carson, 2008: 64)

These successful coaches did not treat the teaching of life skills as a separate activity from their general coaching duties (Gould and Carson, 2008).

Coaching strategies

Some youth sport coaches rely on specific strategies to facilitate youth development, while others struggle in articulating how they promote the development of their athletes in practice (Camiré, Trudel, and Forneris, 2014). There is therefore a perceived need to help sport coaches integrate some psychological skills in their coaching practice (Camiré and Trudel, 2014).

With regards to specific *coaching strategies*, Camiré, Forneris, Trudel, and Bernard (2011) identified five strategies for facilitating youth development outcomes: (1) carefully developing a coaching philosophy; (2) developing meaningful relationships with athletes; (3) intentionally planning developmental strategies in coaching practice; (4) talking about and getting athletes to practise life skills, including organizing tangible learning opportunities; and (5) teaching athletes how to transfer life skills to non-sport settings. They added that coaches must aim to increase youth's confidence in using their skills in life situation outside the sport.

Finally, it seems that the leadership style of coaches and other facilitators is also an important factor. Several studies suggest that a transformative leadership approach is more conducive than others to positive psychosocial outcomes among youth who participate in a sport-based programme (Morgan and Bush, 2016; Turnnidge and Côté, 2018; Newland et al, 2019). It is a follower-based approach, where leaders help followers to achieve their potential, by acting as role models, inspiring, and empowering followers, while holding them to high expectations and expressing care and concern for the followers and recognizing their individual needs. A study of the relationships between athletes' perceptions of coach transformative leadership and PYD confirmed that a coach's transformational leadership is associated with greater positive development outcomes (that is, the 5Cs – Competence, Confidence, Connection, Character, and Caring) (Newland et al, 2019).

Figure 7.1 summarizes research findings on coaching success (Gould and Carson, 2008; Camiré et al, 2011; Flett et al, 2013; Bean et al, 2018), which are consistent with what we have heard about successful coaches during our own interviews. More specifically, this illustrates how successful coaching characteristics and strategies apply to the different levels of implicit/explicit continuum of life skills development and transfer. This could potentially be used to inform uniform principles for the training of coaches and to help to properly structure and plan programmes.

Training

Research on the effectiveness of sport-based youth development and crime prevention programmes emphasizes the importance of capacity building and the need to invest in developing and supporting key human resources, in particular coaches, volunteers, and other facilitators. Support staff and educators may complement the role of coaches in promoting positive development and are sometimes in a better position to impart and help the transfer of life skills in sport-based positive development programmes in high school sports, and in community-based programmes (Lim, Koh, and Chan, 2019). Therefore, much of what follows in this chapter is applicable to everyone who plays a role in developing, managing, and delivering a sport-based PYD crime prevention programme.

There already are programmes for teaching coaches how to intentionally include a PYD approach (Santos, Strachan, and Pereira, 2019). There is one manual on life skills training through sport to prevent crime and to reduce violence and drug use that has been developed for the delivery of a specific programme (United Nations Office on Drugs and Crime, 2017). There are also hundreds of coach development programmes (CDPs) with different focuses, objectives, and methods. Only a few of them focus on PYD and the role of coaches in promoting it (Lefebvre et al, 2016). Jennifer Turnnidge and Jean Côté, of Queens University (Kingston, Ontario), have developed an evidence-informed CDP based on the transformational leadership (TFL) theory: the *Transformational Coaching Workshop* (Turnnidge and Côté, 2017). They also suggested some practical strategies for its implementation.

Locally, however, an assessment of local training needs and resources may help develop and deliver training programmes

Figure 7.1: Life skills development and coaching strategies

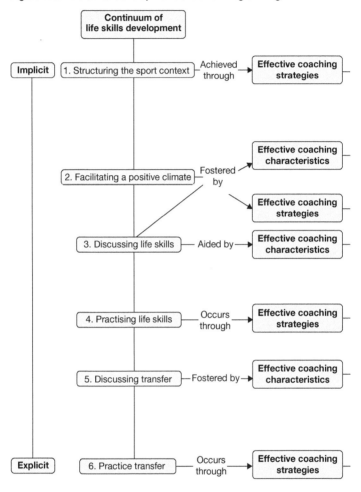

that can boost the capacity of existing sport-based programmes and encourage the development of more effective ones. Key elements of such training are likely to include:

• awareness of the importance of nurturing quality coach–youth relationships;

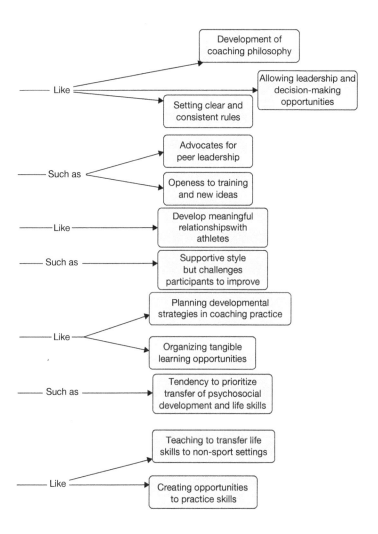

- how to intentionally include a positive development element in their approach with youth (Santos, Strachan, and Pereira, 2019);
- how to use interpersonal behaviours that respond to the youth's basic psychological needs;

- strategies to facilitate the transfer of life skills (Camiré et al, 2011; Camiré, Trudel, and Formeris, 2014; Camiré, Trudel, and Bernard, 2013);
- transformational coaching;
- motivational approaches (the role of intrinsic motivation);
- how to instill a philosophy of non-violence and encourage self-control, self-confidence, responsibility, and respect for oneself and others;
- gender-sensitive and culturally relevant coaching strategies (Fagan and Lindsey, 2014; Lipowski et al, 2016);
- how to respond to conflict and help youth learn how to prevent and resolve conflict (Hemphill et al, 2018; Jacobs, Wahl-Alexander and Mack, 2019);
- awareness of programme attrition issues and ideas for alternative strategies that are developmentally sensitive and effective (Flett, Gould, and Lauer, 2012);
- key considerations for developing meaningful and inclusive sport-based programmes for vulnerable groups and youth from various ethnocultural backgrounds.

Assessment tools are already available for research and programme development purposes. The Coaching Behaviour Assessment System (CBAS) has been used in several studies to examine coaches' influence on children's psychological development through sport. A team of Canadian researchers has also developed and initially validated a scale that can be used to measure the extent to which coaches intentionally teach life skills through sport (the Coaching for Life Skills Questionnaire) (Camiré et al, 2021). The tool was used to evaluate a Coaching for Life Skills online training programme (Camiré et al, 2020).

Key research findings

The following summarizes some key findings of recent research on the role and practices of sport coaches, facilitators, and volunteers involved in sport-based positive development programmes.

Intentional teaching and transfer of life skills

The practice of life skills is more conducive to development than the mere discussion of life skills (Holt et al, 2017). Coaches must look for opportunities for youth to practise skills outside of the sport context. They can also intentionally create opportunities for youth to practise life skills and transfer them to other contexts (Bean et al, 2018). Coaches therefore require specific training on how to intentionally integrate life skills into their regular coaching practice (Bean and Forneris, 2017).

Awareness

Coaches must understand that life skills transfer is not an automatic process and that it must be reinforced continuously in an explicit manner. For example, 'whenever teachable moments presented themselves, coaches took advantage of them to talk to their athletes about the transferability of life skills and provided athletes concrete examples of situations and contexts in which life skills can be transferred' (Camiré et al, 2011: 97). Coaches should also be aware of the impact of their own behaviour as a role model to maximize the potential of sport-based interventions (Spruit et al, 2018b). Their influence is optimized when they remain sensitive and responsive to developmental needs and signal their openness to discussing them with youth (Spruit et al, 2018b).

Relationships and leadership

There is no doubt that meaningful relationships and interactions between youth and adults are crucial to foster young people's development through sport (Crabbe, 2007; Debognies et al, 2019). The best predictor of developmental experiences is a combination of the quality of the coach–youth relationship and a coach's transformational leadership behaviour (Vella, Oades, and Crowe, 2013). A clear link can be observed between coaches' leadership styles and PYD. Coaches' transformational leadership is associated with an impact on positive psychosocial development outcomes in the youth participating in a sport-based programme (Vella, Oades, and Crowe, 2013; Morgan and Bush, 2016; Turnnidge and Côté, 2017, 2018; Newland et al, 2019). The most influential leadership behaviours are individual consideration, intellectual stimulation, and appropriate role modelling (Vella, Oades, and Crowe, 2011, 2013).

Several factors typically play a role in how coaches build relationships that can instigate personal development for young people in disadvantaged situations. Debognies and colleagues listed some of these factors: (a) there should be enough time for the relationship to develop; (b) coaches and staff must remain authentic; (c) expertise is equalized; (d) adhering strictly to a non-judgemental approach; (e) reliance on the coach's own cultural capital; (f) co-organizing activities with other groups with similar objectives; (g) adopting a 'thousand chances' response to youth behaviour and efforts; and, (h) providing individual support (Debognies et al, 2019).

Role models

Coaches, parents, and referees, especially in competitive games, can influence players' behaviour, learning, and socialization. Their actions affect the players' learning and communicate what is regarded as important and valuable. 'The pedagogical function of parents, coaches and referees is of key importance in the co-creation of educational practices' (Andersson, 2019: 617). Coaches and other programme staff members must be capable of developing a relationship of trust with the youth. They must be able to understand the world the youth live in but, at the same time, must be able to set limits (Schwenzer et al, 2007: 42).

Coaching strategies

Positive development outcomes are more likely to be developed through sport-based programmes when coaches are able to create safe and suitable environments (Camiré, Trudel, and Formeris, 2012). By using specific practical strategies and reinforcing the parallels between sport and life, coaches can heighten the potential of sport as a tool for youth development (Camiré et al, 2011).

Coaching life skills is a mindset as well as a specific activity (Gould and Carson, 2008). Coaches and other programme staff members who are perceived by youth as emotionally supportive and autonomy supportive can increase the youth's motivation to participate fully in the programme and help them to improve their self-confidence and self-control (Riley et al, 2017). An 'autonomy-supportive' approach to coaching, focused on developing youth's autonomy, competence, and relatedness, is superior to a 'controlling' approach in terms of fostering youth development (Cowan et al, 2012). Involving athletes and participants in decision-making processes is crucial for maintaining adaptive motivation and positive consequences (Cowan et al, 2012).

Authority: affirmation of values and enforcement of rules

Coaches and other programme staff should work with specific values and define the meaning of them to participants (Camiré and Trudel, 2010). Concrete and proactive interventions are required from the coaches to reduce incidences of gamesmanship and re-emphasize the development of moral character in sport (Camiré and Trudel, 2010).

The coaches' authority relationship with youth is viewed as a key didactical proficiency of coaches and a crucial aspect of successful programmes. Providing a rule-based setting and a safe sport environment requires coaches who have the authority to put rules into practice (Haudenhuyse, Theeboom, and Coalter, 2012). Enforcing behavioural rules may not be limited to behaviour during the programme activities but may extend to behaviour outside of these activities. Additionally, it is important that coaches safeguard and promote referee respect among the players. Coaches can safeguard a referee's authority in relation to the players by being friendly, polite, balanced, and positive; supporting difficult decisions, and intervening when players complain and argue with a referee (Andersson, 2019). Finally, coaches' behaviour and programme activities should be carefully monitored and supervised to avoid situations involving harmful behaviour or practices (De Wet, Muloiwa and Odimegwu, 2018).

Responsiveness to age and gender

The age and gender of participants in sport-based PYD programmes are relevant to coaching approaches and techniques. For example, coaching young children should focus less on how to win games, since most of them do not have the physical, emotional, mental, or social capacity to perform at the coach's expected level (Flett, Gould, and Lauer, 2012).

Some sport-based interventions may have different, and sometimes opposite, effects on male and female participants (Fagan and Lindsey, 2014). It is therefore important to ensure that the interventions address the risk and protective factors that are most salient for each gender group. It is also important to recruit female coaches and facilitators and to develop a capacity among facilitators, coaches, trainers, and sports leaders to act as positive role models and challenge gender stereotypes, norms, and attitudes that condone or justify gender-based discrimination and violence.

Positive development in the elite sport context

Coaches can facilitate youth development in the context of elite competitive sports (for example, hockey or football), but the context sometimes makes their role more complex. Coaches often demonstrate behaviours that can potentially facilitate youth development, but the sport structure (that is, a professional sports model that focuses on competition and performance from early childhood) often restricts their ability to do so. In some instances, the coach's own motivations to achieve performance success presented a challenge to fostering youth development (Preston, Allan, and Fraser-Thomas, 2021).

EIGHT

Crime Prevention Outcomes and Implications for Future Investments

This chapter concludes the book with a discussion of the place of sports in overall crime prevention strategies and whether further investments in sport-based crime prevention programmes are justified. The coincidence of popular interest in sport-based crime prevention programmes and the limited empirical evidence on their impacts underscores the need for further research. At this point, although there is useful knowledge about what can increase the positive development aspects of a sport-based programme, it remains very difficult to know for whom sport-based crime prevention interventions are most effective and what they should consist of. Definitive conclusions are still not possible about what, if anything, can make sport-based interventions more effective in preventing crime or violence (Spruit et al, 2018a). That drawback points to the critical need for substantial and rigorous evaluations.

There is still a need to isolate and understand both the protective and the negative influences of sports on youth crime and to plan interventions so that negative influences can be confined or mitigated (Spruit et al, 2016). It stands to reason that '[t]he most successful sport-related programmes and projects are those which understand what is possible and clearly articulate and implement what they are trying to achieve. Resources should not be allocated to projects which make unqualified claims relating to their capacity to impact upon specific social outcomes. (Crabbe et al, 2006: 4)

Sport-based crime prevention programmes are rarely evaluated and, when they are, the evaluations are methodologically weak and overly simplistic in their theorizing about the causes of youth crime (Bailey, 2005). Based on the present review, it appears that none of the sport-based crime prevention programmes in British Columbia have been evaluated or empirically reviewed and none have formulated a clear theory of change or logic model that directly links activities to crime prevention. It was not even clear that any of these programmes were committed to achieving specific or measurable crime prevention outcomes, and programme leaders did not appear particularly interested in participating in an evaluation of their programme. This is not unique to British Columbia. Yet, one should still ask whether the available evidence of their crime prevention effectiveness justifies investments of crime prevention funds, and whether investments in other programmes may not yield far more important results. Sports are very popular and sport-based crime prevention programmes compete, perhaps unfairly, with other programmes that are more likely to produce crime prevention outcomes.

For at least two decades, there have been calls for rigorous evaluations of sport-based programmes established for the explicit purpose of crime prevention (Cameron and MacDougall, 2000). The lack of robust evaluations and ongoing monitoring of these programmes has hampered progress towards more effective interventions.

Crime prevention outcomes

There is evidence of the beneficial effects of sport participation. However, as discussed in previous chapters, the question of whether sport participation promotes or inhibits problem behaviours remains unresolved. For example, a longitudinal study analyzed the direction of the association between sport participation and problem behaviour among a nationally representative sample of 1,692 adolescents (ages 11–19) in the US (Sheppard and Mahoney, 2012). The study found that externalizing behaviour was not related to time spent in sport. It also suggested that other intervening factors, such as context, prior youth experience, type of sport, and related activities, are also at play.

Measuring the impact of any crime prevention programme can be challenging, even if some progress has been made in addressing various theoretical and methodological issues (Elliott and Fagan, 2017). Notwithstanding these challenges, criminology and the crime prevention field must remain committed to evidence-based crime prevention programming and should not shy away from measuring the impact of sport-based crime prevention programmes, irrespective of their enduring public popularity.

Programmes should be consistently evaluated using objective measures with a focus on identifying specific factors that prompt behavioural change and promote crime reduction, while also accounting for structural, social, and community factors and circumstances rather than just individual factors (Nichols, 1997; Cameron and MacDougall, 2000; Catalano et al, 2002; Coakley, 2002; Hartman and Depro, 2006; Chamberlain, 2013; Armour and Sandford, 2013; Roth and Brooks-Gunn, 2016). Non-sport measures are also needed to test what has changed in the lives of participating youth and whether – and, if so, why – this is linked to a reduction of juvenile delinquency (Spruit et al, 2018a).

However, since existing research has already established that sports programmes on their own are unlikely to yield crime prevention outcomes and must be accompanied by other interventions, evaluations of sport-based crime prevention programmes will continue to face the problem of effect attribution. It is incumbent on researchers to find ways to distinguish between the effect of sport participation and that of other accompanying interventions. Since it is often suggested that sports merely function as a 'hook' to get youth's attention and engage them in other positive development activities, researchers must ask for whom is sport an effective 'hook' and whether other popular youth activities could play the same role or provide a more inclusive and effective means to engage youth at risk. Future research should refine existing categorizations of sport-based programmes and attempt to quantify the specific outcomes attributable to sport participation among other related crime prevention outcomes observed in multi-component sport-based programmes.

There are also practical and methodological difficulties in measuring the impact of a particular sport-based crime prevention programme as distinct from the collective impact of simultaneous crime prevention initiatives targeting the same youth or community. Since sport-based interventions are expected to be but one aspect of a broader crime prevention strategy, it is sometimes impossible to disentangle their impact from that of other elements of that strategy.

Lastly, evaluations of sport-based crime prevention programmes tend to show high levels of satisfaction among participants, who typically agree that they have learned useful life skills (Mason, Cleland, and Aldridge, 2017). Qualitative interviews with youth who participate in sport-based programmes tend to offer a spontaneously positive view of their benefits (Meek, 2014). Given the difficulty of measuring any impact of a small sport-based programme on the youth's criminal involvement (let alone crime rates) and since most programmes involve a small number of participants (youth or at-risk youth), evaluations often rely on self-reported delinquency.

The crime reduction outcomes of sport-based interventions remain inherently difficult to measure. It may be, as McNeill suggested, that 'one of criminology's failings, perhaps, has been to use evaluation approaches that settle for measuring the absence of negative outcomes – like reoffending – rather than the achievement of positive social goods' (McNeill,

2021: 39). Certainly, outside criminology, research on sport-based positive youth development is contributing to a broader understanding of the outcomes to be measured. Nevertheless, since many of these programmes are funded out of crime prevention budgets, one cannot entirely escape the question of whether they contribute to preventing youth crime. Further crime prevention investments in these types of programmes deserve more rigorous evaluations. However, such evaluations require far more resources than those usually available to these programmes (Nichols and Crow, 2004).

Notes

three Sports and Secondary Crime Prevention: Youth at Risk

[1] *Social responsibility* refers to attitudes and initiatives to respect the rights of others, being a responsible citizen, and avoiding violent and destructive behaviours.

[2] Five core competencies: (1) positive sense of self, (2) self control, (3) decision-making skills, (4) a moral system of belief, and (5) prosocial connectedness.

[3] For example, in the United States, the National Association of Police Athletic/Activities Leagues, Inc supports community-based youth sports and athletics activities as a means to develop better relationships with the community and trust-building strategies between the police and the community, https://www.nationalpal.org/

five Theory of Change Underlying Sport-Based Programmes

[1] Given that theories of desistance are attempting to explain adult behaviour, adjustments will obviously have to be made when dealing with other groups, such as youth and young people in this case. However, certain core principles and concepts from these theories are still relevant.

[2] Given Moffitt's (1993) finding about the normality of deviant and delinquent behaviour and what is known about the state of drift, it may be unrealistic to expect full desistance from all criminal activity. Instead, a reasonable expectation might be the formation of negative attitudes about crimes that have clear victims and harm others.

References

Agans, J.P., Davis, J.L., Vazou, S., and Jarus, T. (2019) 'Self-determination through circus arts: exploring youth development in a novel activity context', *Journal of Youth Development*, 14(3): 110–129.

Albertson, K. and Hall, L. (2020) 'Building social capital to encourage desistance', in P. Ugwudike, H. Graham, F. McNeill, P. Raynor, F. Taxman, and C. Trotter (eds), *The Routledge Companion to Rehabilitative Work in Criminal Justice*, Abingdon: Routledge, pp 310–319.

Alexander, K., Stafford, A., and Lewis, R. (2011) *The Experiences of Children Participating in Organised Sport in the UK*, London: NSPCC.

Allen, G. and Rhind, D. (2019) 'Taught not caught: exploring male adolescent experiences of explicitly transferring life skills from the sports hall into the classroom', *Qualitative Research in Sport, Exercise and Health*, 11(2): 188–200.

Allison, K.W., Edmonds, T., Wilson, K., Pope, M., and Farrell, A.D. (2011) 'Connecting youth violence prevention, positive youth development, and community mobilization', *American Journal of Community Psychology*, 18(8): 8–20.

Amemiya, J., Kieta, J., and Monahan, K.C. (2017) 'Adolescent offenders' qualitative reflections on desistance from crime', *Journal of Research on Adolescence*, 27(4): 765–781.

Amtmann, J. and Kukay, J. (2016) 'Fitness changes after an 8-week fitness coaching program at a regional youth detention facility', *Journal of Correctional Health Care*, 22(1): 75–83.

Anderson, A. (2017) 'The five-factor model for leisure management: pedagogies for assessing personality differences in positive youth development programmes', *World Leisure Journal*, 59(1): 70–76.

Andersson, E. (2019) 'A referee perspective on the educational practice of competitive youth games: exploring the pedagogical function of parents, coaches and referees in grassroots soccer', *Physical Education and Sport Pedagogy*, 24(6): 615–628.

Andrews, J.P. and Andrews, G.J. (2003) 'Life in a secure unit: the rehabilitation of young people through the use of sport', *Social Science & Medicine*, 56(3): 531–550.

Armour, K. and Duncombe, R. (2012) 'Changing lives? Critical evaluation of a school-based athlete role model intervention', *Sport, Education, and Society*, 17(3): 381–403.

Armour, K. and Sandford, R. (2013) 'Positive youth development through an outdoor physical activity programme: evidence from a four-year evaluation', *Educational Review*, 65(1): 85–108.

Armour, K., Sandford, R., and Duncombe, R. (2013) 'Positive youth development and physical activity/sport interventions: mechanisms leading to sustained impact', *Physical Education and Sport Pedagogy*, 18(3): 256–281.

Armstrong, D. (2004) 'A risky business? Research, policy, governmentality and youth offending', *Youth Justice*, 4(2): 100–116.

Armstrong, D. (2006) 'Becoming criminal: the cultural politics of risk', *International Journal of Inclusive Education*, 10(2–3): 265–278.

Astbury, R., Knight, B., and Nichols, G. (2005) 'The contribution of sport-related interventions to the long-term development of disaffected young people: an evaluation of the Fairbridge program', *Journal of Park and Recreation Administration*, 23(3): 82–98.

Bailey, R. (2005) 'Evaluating the relationship between physical education, sport and social inclusion', *Educational Review*, 57(1): 71–90.

Bailey, R. (2018) 'Sport, physical education and educational worth', *Educational Review*, 70(1): 51–66.

Barret, C.J. (2017) 'Mindfulness and rehabilitation: teaching yoga and meditation to young men in an alternative to incarceration program', *International Journal of Offender Therapy and Comparative Criminology*, 61(15): 1719–1738.

Bartels, L., Oxman, L.M., and Hopkins, A. (2019) '"I would just feel really relaxed and at peace": findings from a pilot prison yoga program in Australia', *International Journal of Offender Therapy and Comparative Criminology*, 63(15–16): 2531–2549.

Basto-Pereira, M. and Farrington, D.P. (2020) 'Lifelong conviction pathways and self-reported offending: towards a deeper comprehension of criminal career development', *British Journal of Criminology*, 60(2): 285–302.

Basto-Pereira, M., Queiroz-Garcia, I., Maciel, L., Leal, I., and Gouveia-Pereira, M. (2020) 'An international study of pro/antisocial behavior in young adults', *Cross-Cultural Research*, 54(1): 92–105.

Bean, C., Fortier, M., Post, C., and Chima, K. (2014) 'Understanding how organized youth sport may be harming individual players within the family unit: a literature review', *International Journal of Environmental Research and Public Health*, 11(10): 10226–10268.

Bean, C. and Forneris, T. (2016) 'Examining the importance of intentionally structuring the youth sport context to facilitate positive youth development', *Journal of Applied Sport Psychology*, 28(4): 410–425.

Bean, C. and Forneris, T. (2017) 'Is life skill development a by-product of sport participation? Perceptions of youth sport coaches', *Journal of Applied Sport Psychology*, 29(2): 234–250.

Bean, C. and Forneris, T. (2019) 'Examining the role of needs support in mediating the relationship between program quality and psychosocial outcomes in youth sport', *International Journal of Sport and Exercise Psychology*, 17(4): 350–366.

Bean, C., Kendellen, K., and Forneris, T. (2016) 'Moving beyond the gym: exploring life skill transfer within a female physical activity-based life skills program', *Journal of Applied Sport Psychology*, 28(3): 274–290.

Bean, C., Kramers, S., Forneris, T., and Camiré, M. (2018) 'The implicit/explicit continuum of life skills development and transfer', *Quest*, 70(4): 456–479.

Bean, C., Solstad, B.E., Ivarsson, A., and Forneris, T. (2020) 'Longitudinal associations between perceived programme quality, basic needs support and basic needs satisfaction within youth sport: a person-centred approach', *International Journal of Sport and Exercise Psychology*, 18(1): 76–92.

Bean, C., McFadden, T., Fortier, M., and Forneris, T. (2021) 'Understanding the relationships between programme quality, psychological needs satisfaction, and mental well-being in competitive youth sport', *International Journal of Sport and Exercise Psychology*, 19(2): 246–264.

Beelmann, A. and Lösel, F. (2021) 'A comprehensive meta-analysis of randomized evaluations of the effect of child social skills training on antisocial development', *Journal of Developmental and Life-Course Criminology*, 7(1): 41–65.

Berdychevsky, L., Stodolska, M., and Shinew, K.J. (2022) 'The roles of recreation in the prevention, intervention and rehabilitation programs addressing youth gang involvement and violence', *Leisure Sciences*, 44(3): 343–365.

Berry, V., Little, M., Axford, N., and Cusick, G.R. (2009) 'An evaluation of youth at risk's coaching for communities programme', *The Howard Journal of Criminal Justice*, 48(1): 60–75.

Bjørnseth, I. and Szabo, A. (2018) 'Sexual violence against children in sports and exercise: a systematic literature review', *Journal of Child Sexual Abuse*, 27(4): 365–385.

Boivin, R. and Morselli, C. (2016) *Les Réseaux Criminels*, Montréal: Les Presses de l'Université de Montréal.

Bradshaw, C.P., O'Brennan, L.M., and McNeely, C.A. (2008) 'Core competencies and the prevention of school failure and early school leaving', in N.G. Guerra and C.P. Bradshaw (eds), *Core Competencies to Prevent Problem Behaviors and Promote Positive Youth Development*, New York, NY: Wiley, pp 19–32.

Brezina, T. and Aragones, A.A. (2004) 'Devils in disguise: the contribution of positive labeling to "sneaky thrills" delinquency', *Deviant Behavior*, 25(6): 513–535.

Brosens, D., Dury, S., Vertonghen, J., Vert, D., and De Ponder, L. (2017) 'Understanding the barriers to prisoners' participation in sports activities', *The Prison Journal*, 97(2): 181–201.

Brosnan, S. (2020) 'The impact of sports participation on crime in England between 2012 and 2015', *Sport in Society*, 23(6): 1080–1090.

Brunelle, J., Danish, S.J., and Forneris, T. (2007) 'The impact of a sport-based life skill program on adolescent prosocial values', *Applied Developmental Science*, 11(1): 43–55.

Bruner, M.W., Balish, S.M., Forrest, C., Brown, S., Webber, K., Gray, E., McGuckin, M. Keats, M.R., Rehman, L., and Shields, C.A. (2017) 'Ties that bond: youth sport as a vehicle for social identity and positive youth development', *Research Quarterly for Exercise and Sport*, 88(2): 209–214.

Bruner, M.W., Hillier, S., Baillie, C.P.T., Lavallée, L.F., Bruner, B.G., Hare, K., Lovelace, R., and Lévesque, L. (2016) 'Positive youth development in aboriginal physical activity and sport: a systematic review', *Adolescent Research Review*, 1(3): 257–269.

Buelens, E., Theeboom, M., Vertonghen, J., and Martelaer, K.D. (2015) 'Socially vulnerable youth and volunteering in sports: analyzing a Brussels training program for young soccer coaches', *Social Inclusion*, 3(3): 82–97.

Buelens, E., Theeboom, M., Vertonghen, J., and Martelaer, K.D. (2017) 'Conditions for successfully increasing disadvantaged adolescents' engagement in the development through volunteering in community sport', *Social Inclusion*, 5(2): 179–197.

Caldwell, L.L. and Smith, E.A. (2006) 'Leisure as a context for youth development and delinquency prevention', *Australian and New Zealand Journal of Criminology*, 39(3): 398–418.

Cameron, M. and MacDougall, C.J. (2000) 'Crime prevention through sport and physical activity', *Trends & Issues in Crime and Criminal Justice*, 165: 1–6.

Camiré, M. (2015) 'Reconciling competition and positive youth development in sport', *Staps 2015/3*, 109: 25–39.

Camiré, M. and Trudel, P. (2010) 'High school athletes' perspectives on character development through sport participation', *Physical Education and Sport Pedagogy*, 15(2): 193–207.

Camiré, M. and Trudel, P. (2014) 'Helping youth sport coaches integrate psychological skills in their coaching practice', *Qualitative Research in Sport, Exercise and Health*, 6(4): 617–634.

Camiré, M., Trudel, P. and Forneris, T. (2012) 'Coaching and transferring life skills: philosophies and strategies used by model high school coaches', *Sport Psychologist*, 26(2): 243–260.

Camiré, M., Trudel, P., and Bernard, D. (2013) 'A case study of a high school sport program: designed to teach athletes life skills and values', *The Sport Psychologist*, 27(2): 188–200.

Camiré, M., Trudel, P., and Forneris, T. (2014) 'Examining how model youth sport coaches learn to facilitate positive youth development', *Physical Education and Sport Pedagogy*, 19(1): 1–17.

Camiré, M., Forneris, T., Trudel, P., and Bernard, D. (2011) 'Strategies for helping coaches facilitate positive youth development through sport', *Journal of Sport Psychology in Action*, 2: 92–99.

Camiré, M., Kendellen, K., Rathwell, S., and Turgeon, S. (2020) 'Evaluating the coaching for life skills online training program: a randomised controlled trial', *Psychology of Sport and Exercise*, 48. 101649: 1–11.

Camiré, M., Turgeon, S., Kramers, S., Rathwell, S., Bean, C., Sabourin, C., and Pierce, P. (2021) 'Development and initial validation of the coaching life skills in sport questionnaire', *Psychology of Sport and Exercise*, 53, 101845.

Carlsson, C. (2013) 'Masculinities, persistence, and desistance', *Criminology*, 51(3): 661–693.

Case, S. (2007) 'Questioning the "evidence" of risk that underpins evidence-led youth justice interventions', *Youth Justice*, 7(2): 91–105.

Case, S. and Haines, K. (2009) *Understanding Youth Offending: Risk Factor Research, Policy and Practice*, Cullompton: Willan Publishing.

Case, S. and Haines, K. (2010) 'Risky business? The risk in risk factor research', *Criminal Justice Matters*, 80(1): 20–22.

Case, S. and Haines, K. (2021) 'Abolishing youth justice systems: children first, offenders nowhere', *Youth Justice*, 21(1): 3–17.

Catalano, R.F., Berglund, M.L., Ryan, J.A.M., Lonczak, H.S., and Hawkins, J.D. (2002) 'Positive youth development in the United States: research findings on evaluations of positive youth development programs', *The Annals of the American Academy of Political and Social Science*, 591(1): 98–124.

Catalano, R.F. and Hawkins, J.D. (1996) 'The social development model: a theory of anti-social behaviour', in J. Hawkins (ed.) Delinquency and Crime: Current Theories, pp. 149–97. Cambridge: Cambridge University Press, pp 149–197.

Chamberlain, J.M. (2013) 'Sports-based intervention and the problem of youth offending: a diverse enough tool for a diverse society?', Sport in Society, 16(10), 1279–1292.

Chinkov, A.E. and Holt, N.L. (2016) 'Implicit transfer of life skills through participation in Brazilian jiu-jitsu, Journal of Applied Sport Psychology, 28: 139–153.

Coakley, J. (1998) Sport in Society: Issues and Controversies, Boston, MA: McGraw Hill.

Coakley, J. (2002) 'Using sports to control deviance and violence among youths: let's be critical and cautious', in M. Gatz, M.A. Messner, and S.J. Ball-Rokeach (eds), Paradoxes of Youth and Sport, New York, NY: University of New York Press, pp 13–30.

Coakley, J. (2011) 'Youth sports: what counts as "positive development"?', Journal of Sport and Social Issues, 35(3): 306–324.

Coalter, F. (2006) Sport-in-Development: A Monitoring and Evaluation Manual, London: UK Sport.

Coalter, F. (2007) A Wider Social Role for Sport: Who's Keeping the Score?, New York, NY: Routledge.

Coalter, F. (2010a) 'Sport-for-development: going beyond the boundary?', Sport in Society, 13(9): 1374–1391.

Coalter, F. (2010b) 'The politics of sport-for-development: limited focus programmes and broad-gauge problems?', International Review for the Sociology of Sport, 45(3): 295–314.

Coalter, F. (2013a) '"There is loads of relationships here": developing a programme theory for sport-for-change programmes', International Review for the Sociology of Sport, 48(5): 594–612.

Coalter, F. (2013b) Sport for Development: What Game Are We Playing?, London: Routledge.

Collins, K., Gould, D.R., Lauer, L., and Chung, Y. (2009) 'Coaching life skills through football: philosophical beliefs of outstanding high school football coaches', International Journal of Coaching Science, 3(1): 16–37.

Collins, M. (2010) 'From "sport for good" to "sport for sport's sake"': not a good move for sports development in England?', *International Journal of Sport Policy and Politics*, 2(3): 367–379.

Collins, M.F. and Kay, T. (2014) *Sport and Social Exclusion* (2nd edn), New York, NY: Routledge.

Colvin, M., Cullen, F.T., and Vander Ven, T. (2002) 'Coercion, social support, and crime: an emerging theoretical consensus', *Criminology*, 40: 19–42.

Copp, J.E., Giordano, P.C., Longmore, M.A., and Manning W.D. (2020) 'Desistance from crime during the transition to adulthood: the influence of parents, peers, and shifts in identity', *Journal of Research in Crime and Delinquency*, 57(3): 294–332.

Coppola, A.M., Holt, N.L., and McHugh, T-L.F. (2020) 'Supporting indigenous youth activity programmes: a community-based participatory research approach', *Qualitative Research in Sport, Exercise and Health*, 12(3): 319–335.

Copus, R. and Laqueur, H. (2019) 'Entertainment as crime prevention: evidence from Chicago sports games', *Journal of Sports Economics*, 20(3): 344–370.

Côté, J. and Gilbert, W. (2009) 'An integrative definition of coaching effectiveness and expertise', *International Journal of Sports Science & Coaching*, 4(3): 307–323.

Côté, J. and Hancock, D.J. (2016) 'Evidence-based policies for youth sport programmes', *International Journal of Sport Policy and Politics*, 8(1): 51–65.

Côté, J., Coakley, C., and Bruner, M.W. (2011) 'Children's talent development in sport: effectiveness or efficiency?, in S. Dagkas and K. Armour (eds). *Inclusion and Exclusion Through Youth Sport*. London: Routledge, 172–185.

Côté, J., Strachan, L., and Fraser-Thomas, J. (2008) 'Participation, personal development and performance through youth sport', in N. L. Holt (Ed.), *Positive Youth Development Through Sport*. New York, New York: Routledge, 34–45.

Council of Europe, Committee of Ministers (2006) Recommendation Rec (2006) 2 of the Committee of Ministers to member states on the European Prison Rules. Available from: http://www.refwo rld.org/docid/43f3134810.html

Cowan, D. and Taylor, I.M. (2016) ' "I'm proud of what I achieved; I'm also ashamed of what I done": a soccer coach's tale of sport, status, and criminal behaviour', *Qualitative Research in Sport, Exercise and Health*, 8(5): 505–518.

Cowan, T., Taylor, I.M., McEwan, H.E., and Baker, J.S. (2012) 'Bridging the gap between self-determination theory and coaching soccer to disadvantaged youth', *Journal of Applied Sport Psychology*, 24: 361–374.

Crabbe, T. (2000) 'A sporting chance: using sport to tackle drug use and crime', *Drugs: Education, Prevention & Policy*, 7(4): 381–391.

Crabbe, T. (2007) 'Reaching the "hard to reach": engagement, relationships building and social control in sport based social inclusion work', *International Journal of Sport Management and Marketing*, 2(1–2): 27–40.

Crabbe, T., Bailey, G., Blackshaw, T., Adam, B., Choak, C., Gidley, B., Mellor, G., O'Connor. K., Slater. I., and Woodhouse, D. (2006) *Knowing the Score: Positive Futures Case Study Final Report*, Swindon: Positive Future Team and Crime Concern.

Cullen, F.T. (1994) 'Social support as an organizing concept for criminology: presidential address to the Academy of Criminal Justice Sciences', *Justice Quarterly*, 11(4): 527–559.

Curran, T. and Wexler, L. (2017) 'School-based positive youth development: a systematic review of the literature', *Journal of School Health*, 87(1): 71–80.

Cushion, C. and Partington, M. (2016) 'A critical analysis of the conceptualisation of "coaching philosophy"', *Sport, Education and Society*, 21(6): 851–867.

D'Angelo, D. (2019) 'Sport and integration of migrants: some considerations', *Journal of Mediterranean Knowledge*, 4(1): 3–15.

Dagkas, S. (2018) '"Is social inclusion through PE, Sport and PA still a rhetoric?" Evaluating the relationship between physical education, sport and social inclusion', *Educational Review*, 70(1): 67–74.

Danish, S., Forneris, T., Hodge, K., and Heke, I. (2004) 'Enhancing youth development through sport', *World Leisure Journal*, 46(3): 38–49.

Davis, B.S. and Menard, S. (2013) 'Long term impact of youth sports participation on illegal behavior', *The Social Science Journal*, 50(1): 34–44.

de Sousa Ferreira dos Santos, F., Camiré, M., and Henrique da Fonte Campos, P. (2018) 'Youth sport coaches' role in facilitating positive youth development in Portuguese field hockey', *International Journal of Sport and Exercise Psychology*, 16(3): 221–234.

De Wet, N., Muloiwa, T., and Odimegwu, C. (2018) 'Extra-curricular activities and youth risky behaviours in South Africa', *International Journal of Adolescence and Youth*, 23(4): 431–440.

Debognies, P., Schaillee, H., Haudenhuyse, R., and Theeboom, M. (2019) 'Personal development of disadvantaged youth through community sports: a theory-driven analysis of relational strategies', *Sport in Society*, 22(6): 897–918.

Deci, E.L. and Ryan, R.M. (2000) 'The "what" and "why" of goal pursuits: human needs and the self-determination of behavior', *Psychological Inquiry*, 11: 227–268.

Deuchar, R., Sogaard, T.F., Kolind, T., Thylstrup, B., and Wells, L. (2016) '"When you're boxing you don't think so much": pugilism, transitional masculinities and criminal desistance among young Danish gang members', *Journal of Youth Studies*, 19(6): 725–742.

Dickson, K., Melendez-Torres, G.J., Fletcher, A., Hinds, K., Thomas, J., Stansfield, C., Murphy, S., Campbell, R., and Bonell, C. (2018) 'How do contextual factors influence implementation and receipt of positive youth development programs addressing substance use and violence? A qualitative meta-synthesis of process evaluations', *American Journal of Health,* 32(4): 1110–1121.

Doré I., Sabiston C.M., Sylvestre M.-P., Brunet J., O'Loughlin, J., Nader, P.A., Gallant, F., and Bélanger, M. (2019) 'Years participating in sports during childhood predicts mental health in adolescence: a 5-year longitudinal study', *Journal of Adolescent Health,* 64(6):790–796.

Dorsch, T.E., Smith, A.L., and McDonough, M.H. (2009) 'Parents' perceptions of child-to-parent socialization in organized youth sport', *Journal of Sport & Exercise Psychology*, 31(4): 444–468.

Dorsch, T.E., Smith, A.L. and McDonough, M.H. (2015) 'Early socialization of parents through organized youth sport', *Sport, Exercise, and Performance Psychology*, 4(1): 3–18.

Dorsch, T.E., Smith, A.L., Wilson, S.R., and McDonough, M.H. (2015) 'Parent goals and verbal sideline behavior in organized youth sport', *Sport, Exercise, and Performance Psychology*, 4(1): 19–35.

Draper, C.E., Errington, S., Omar, S., and Makhita, S. (2013) 'The therapeutic benefits of sport in the rehabilitation of young sexual offenders: a qualitative evaluation of the Fight with Insight programme', *Psychology of Sport and Exercise*, 14(4): 519–530.

Dudfield, O. and Dingwall-Smith, M. (2015) *Sport for Development and Peace and the 2030 Agenda for Sustainable Development*, London: Commonwealth Secretariat.

Eccles, J., Gootman, J.A., and Appleton, J. (2002) *Community Programs to Promote Youth Development*, Washington, DC: National Academy Press.

Eckholm, D. (2013) 'Sport and crime prevention: individuality and transferability in research', *Journal of Sport for Development*, 1(2): 1–12.

Eckholm, D. (2019) 'Sport as a means of governing social integration: discourses on bridging and bonding social relations', *Sociology of Sport Journal*, 36(2): 152–161.

Ehsani, M., Dehnavi, A., and Heidary, A. (2012) 'The influence of sport and recreation upon crime reduction: a literature review', *International Journal of Academic Research in Business and Social Sciences*, 2(6): 98–104.

Eisman, A., Lee, D.B., Hsieh, H.F., Stoddard, S.A., and Zimmerman, M.A. (2018) 'More than just keeping busy: the protective effects of organized activity participation on violence and substance use among urban youth', *Journal of Youth and Adolescence*, 47(10): 2231–2242.

Eitle, D., Turner, R.J., and Eitle, T. (2003) 'The deterrence hypothesis reexamined: sports participation and substance use among young adults', *Journal of Drug Issues*, 33(1): 193–221.

Elliott, D. and Fagan, A. (2017) *The Prevention of Crime*, Malden, MA: Wiley Blackwell.

Engelberg, T. and Moston, S. (2020) 'Crime and misconduct in sport', *Sport in Society*, 23(6): 975–980.

Evans, B., Eys, M., and Wolf, S. (2013) 'Exploring the nature of interpersonal influence in elite individual sport teams', *Journal of Applied Sport Psychology*, 25(4): 448–462.

Evans, B., Adler, A., MacDonald, D. and Côté, J. (2016) 'Bullying victimization and perpetration among adolescent sport teammates', *Pediatric Exercise Science*, 28(2): 296–303.

Evans, M.B., Allan, V., Erickson, K., Martin, L.J., Budziszewski, R., and Côté, J. (2017) 'Are all sport activities equal? A systematic review of how youth psychosocial experiences vary across differing sport activities', *British Journal of Sports Medicine*, 51(3): 169–176.

F.-Dufour, I., Villeneuve, M.-P. and Perron, C. (2018) 'Les interventions informelles de désistement assisté: une étude de la portée', *Canadian Journal of Criminology and Criminal Justice*, 60(2): 206–240.

Fagan, A. and Lindsey, A.M.L. (2014) 'Gender differences in the effectiveness of delinquency prevention programs: what can be learned from experimental research?', *Criminal Justice and Behavior*, 41(9): 1057–1078.

Farb, A.F. and Matjasko, J. L. (2012) 'Recent advances in research on school-based extracurricular activities and adolescent development', *Developmental Review*, 32(1): 1–48.

Farrall, S. (2019) *The Architecture of Desistance*, Abingdon: Routledge.

Farrington, D.P. (2000) 'Explaining and preventing crime: the globalization of knowledge', *Criminology*, 38(1): 1–24.

Fasting, K., Brackenridge, C., and Sundgot-Borgen, J. (2004) 'Prevalence of sexual harassment among Norwegian female elite athletes in relation to sport type', *International Review for the Sociology of Sport*, 39(4): 373–386.

Fehsenfeld, M. (2015) 'Inclusion of outsiders through sport', *Physical Culture and Sport. Studies & Research*, 65(1): 31–40.

Fernández-Gavira, J., Huete-García, A., and Velez-Colón, L. (2017) 'Vulnerable groups at risk for sport and social exclusion', *Journal of Physical Education and Sport*, 17(1): 312–326.

FIFA (2020) 'Joint Media Release: UNODC, FIFA partner to kick out corruption and foster youth development through football'. Available from: https://www.unodc.org/unodc/press/releases/2020/September/unodc--fifa-partner-to-kick-out-corruption-and-foster-youth-development-through-football.html

Flett, M.R., Gould, D., and Lauer, L. (2012) 'A study of an underserved youth sports program using the youth program quality assessment', *Journal of Applied Sport Psychology*, 24(3): 275–289.

Flett, R.M., Gould, D., Griffes, K.R., and Lauer, L. (2013) 'Tough love for underserved youth: a comparison of more and less effective coaching', *The Sport Psychologist*, 27(4): 325–337.

Fox, C., Grimm, R., and Caldeira, R. (2017) *An Introduction to Evaluation*, London: Sage.

France, A., Freiberg, K. and Homel, R. (2010) 'Beyond risk factors: towards a holistic prevention paradigm for children and young people', *British Journal of Social Work*, 40(4): 1192–1210.

Fraser-Thomas, J. and Côté, J. (2009) 'Understanding adolescents' positive and negative developmental experiences in sport', *The Sport Psychologist*, 23(1): 3–23.

Fraser-Thomas, J.L., Côté, J., and Deakin, J. (2005) 'Youth sport programs: an avenue to foster positive youth development', *Physical Education and Sport Pedagogy*, 10(1): 19–40.

Gadbois, S., Bowker, A.B., Rose-Krasnor, L., and Findlay, L. (2019) 'A qualitative examination of psychologically engaging sport, nonsport, and unstructured activities', *The Sport Psychologist*, 33(2): 97–109.

Gallant, D., Sherry, E., and Nicholson, M. (2015) 'Recreation or rehabilitation? Managing sport for development programs with prison populations', *Sport Management Review*, 18(1): 45–56.

Ganea, V. and Grosu, E.F. (2018) 'Adventure education: a method to prevent antisocial behavior', *Palestrica of the Third Millennium-Civilization and Sport*, 19(2): 116–122.

Garside, R. (2009) 'Risky individuals, risky families or risky societies?', *Criminal Justice Matters*, 78(1): 42–43.

Garst, B.A., Stone, G.A., and Gagnon, R.J. (2016) 'Indoor competition climbing as a context for positive youth development', *Journal of Youth Development*, 11(2): 161102FA003.

Gervis, M., Rhind, D., and Luzar, A. (2016) 'Perceptions of emotional abuse in the coach–athlete relationship in youth sport: the influence of competitive level and outcome', *International Journal of Sports Science & Coaching*, 11(6): 772–779.

Gilchrist, P. and Osborn, G. (2017) 'Risk and benefits in lifestyle sports: parkour, law and social value', *International Journal of Sport Policy and Politics*, 9(1): 55–69.

Gilchrist, P. and Wheaton, B. (2011) 'Lifestyle sport, public policy and youth engagement: examining the emergence of parkour', *International Journal of Sport Policy and Politics*, 3(1): 109–131.

Giordano, S., Cernkovich, S.A., and Rudolph, J.L. (2002) 'Gender, crime, and desistance: toward a theory of cognitive transformation', *The American Journal of Sociology*, 107(4): 990–106.

Giulianotti, R. (2004) 'Human rights, globalization and sentimental education: the case of sport', *Sport in Society*, 7(3): 355–369.

Giulianotti, R. (2011) 'Sport, transnational peacemaking, and global civil society: exploring the reflective discourses of "Sport, Development, and Peace" project officials', *Journal of Sport and Social Issues*, 35(1): 50–71.

Goddard, T. (2014) 'The indeterminacy of the risk factor prevention paradigm: a case study of community partnerships implementing youth and gang violence prevention policy', *Youth Justice*, 14(1): 3–21.

Goddard, T. and Myers, R. (2017) 'Against evidence-based oppression: marginalized youth and the politics of risk-based assessment and intervention', *Theoretical Criminology*, 21(2): 151–167.

Gould, D. and Carson, S. (2008) 'Life skills development through sport: current status and future directions', *International Review of Sport and Exercise Psychology*, 1(1): 58–78.

Gould, D., Flett, R., and Lauer, L. (2012) 'The relationship between psychosocial developmental and the sports climate experienced by underserved youth', *Psychology of Sport and Exercise*, 13(1): 80–87.

Green, K. (2016) 'Tales from the mat: narrating men and meaning making in the mixed martial arts', *Journal of Contemporary Ethnography*, 45(4): 419–450.

Groombridge, N. (2017) *Sports Criminology: A Critical Criminology of Sport and Games*, Bristol: Policy Press.

Gubbles, J., Van der Stouwe, T., Spruit, A., and Stams, G.J.J.M. (2016) 'Martial arts participation and externalizing behaviour in juveniles: a meta-analytic review', *Aggression & Violent Behaviour*, 28: 73–81.

Haines, K. and Case, S. (2008) 'The rhetoric and reality of the "risk factor prevention paradigm" approach to preventing and reducing youth offending', *Youth Justice*, 8(1): 5–20.

Hallinberg, B., Moore, S., Morgan, J., Bowen, K., and Van Goozen, S. (2015) 'Adolescent male hazardous drinking and participation in organised activities: involvement in team sports is associated with less hazardous drinking in young offenders', *Criminal Behaviour and Mental Health*, 25(1): 28–41.

Halsey, M. and Mizzi, J. (2022) 'Co-desistance from crime: Engaging the pro-social dimensions of co-offending', *The British Journal of Criminology*, Advanced publication.

Hartman, D. (2003) 'Theorizing sport as social intervention: a view from the grassroots', *Quest*, 55(2): 118–140.

Hartman, D. and Depro, B. (2006) 'Rethinking sport-based community crime prevention: a preliminary analysis of the relationship between midnight basketball and urban crime rates', *Journal of Sport & Social Issues*, 30(2): 180–196.

Hartmann, D. and Kwauk, C. (2011) 'Sport and development: an overview, critique, and reconstruction, *Journal of Sport & Social Issues*, 35(3): 284–305.

Hartmann-Tews, I. (2021) 'Gender-based violence and organizational silence in voluntary sports organizations', in S. Starystach and K. Höly (eds) *Silence of Organizations: How Organizations Cover up Wrongdoings*, Heidelberg: heiBOOKS, pp 171–194.

Harwood, A., Lavidor, M., and Rassovsky, Y. (2017) 'Reducing aggression with martial arts: a meta-analysis of child and youth studies', *Aggression and Violent Behavior*, 34: 96–101.

Harwood, C.G. and Knight, C.J. (2015) 'Parenting in youth sport: a position paper on parenting expertise', *Psychology of Sport and Exercise*, 16(1): 24–35.

Harwood, C.G., Knight, C.J., Thrower, S.N., and Berrow, S.R. (2019) 'Advancing the study of parental involvement to optimise the psychosocial development and experiences of young athletes', *Psychology of Sport and Exercise*, 42: 66–73.

Haudenhuyse, R.P., Theeboom, M., and Coalter, F. (2012) 'The potential of sport-based social interventions for vulnerable youth: implications for sport coaches and youth workers', *Journal of Youth Studies*, 15(4): 437–454.

Haudenhuyse, R.P., Theeboom, M., and Nols, Z. (2012) 'Sport-based interventions for socially vulnerable youth: towards well-defined interventions with easy-to-follow outcomes?', *International Review for the Sociology of Sport*, 48(4): 471–484.

Haudenhuyse, R.P., Theeboom, M., and Skille, E.A. (2014) 'Towards understanding the potential of sport-based practices for socially vulnerable youth', *Sport in Society*, 17(2): 139–156.

Hazel, N. and Bateman T. (2021) 'Supporting children's resettlement ('reentry') after custody: beyond the risk paradigm', *Youth Justice*, 21(1):71–89.

Heller, S.B., Shah, A.K., Guryan, J., Ludwig, J., Mullainathan, S., and Pollack, H.A. (2017) 'Thinking, fast and slow? Some field experiments to reduce crime and dropout in Chicago', *The Quarterly Journal of Economics*, 132(1): 1–54.

Hellison, D. (2011) *Teaching Personal and Social Responsibility Through Physical Activity* (3rd edn), Champaign, IL: Human Kinetics.

Hemphill, M.A., Gordon, B., and Wright, P.M. (2019) 'Sports as a passport to success: life skill integration in a positive youth development program', *Physical Education and Sport Pedagogy*, 24(4): 390–401.

Hemphill, M.A., Janke, E.M., Gordon, B., and Farrar, H. (2018) 'Restorative youth sports: an applied model for resolving conflicts and building positive relationships', *Journal of Youth Development*, 13(3): 76–96.

Hermens, N., Super, S., Verkooijen, K.T., and Koelen, M.A. (2017) 'A systematic review of life skill development through sports programs serving socially vulnerable youth', *Research Quarterly for Exercise and Sport*, 88(4): 408–424.

Herrmann, J. (2016) *Parkour/Freerunning as a Pathway to Prosocial Change*, Master's thesis, Victoria: University of Wellington. Available from: http://researcharchive.vuw.ac.nz/bitstream/han dle/10063/5096/thesis.pdf?sequence=1

Hodge, C.J., Kanters, M.A., Forneris, T., Bocarro, J.N., and McCord-Sayre, R.A. (2017) 'A family thing: positive youth development outcomes of a sport-based life skills program', *Journal of Park and Recreation Administration*, 35(1): 34–50.

Holt, N. and Tamminen, K. (2009) 'An interpretative analysis of life skills associated with sport participation', *Qualitative Research in Sport and Exercise*, 1(2): 160–175.

Holt, N.L., Tink, L.N., Mandigo, J.L., and Fox, K.R. (2008) 'Do youth learn life skills through their involvement in high school sport? A case study', *Canadian Journal of Education*, 31(2): 281–304.

Holt, N.L., Sehn, Z.L., Spence, J.C., Newton, A., and Ball, G.D.C. (2012) 'Possibilities for positive youth development through physical education and sport programs at an inner-city school', *Physical Education and Sport Pedagogy*, 17(1): 97–11.

Holt, N.L., Neely, K.C., Slater, L.G., Camiré, M., Côté, J., Fraser-Thomas, J., MacDonald, D., Strachan, L., and Tamminen. K.A. (2017) 'A grounded theory of positive youth development through sport based on results from a qualitative meta-study', *International Review of Sport and Exercise Psychology*, 10(1): 1–49.

Hunter, B. and Farrall, S. (2018) 'Emotions, future selves, and the process of desistance', *British Journal of Criminology*, 58(2): 291–308.

Inoue, Y., Wegner, C.E., Jordan, J.S., and Funk, D.C. (2015) 'Relationships between self-determined motivation and developmental outcomes in sport-based positive youth development', *Journal of Applied Sport Psychology*, 27(4): 371–383.

Jacobs, J.M. and Wright, P.M. (2016) 'An alternative application of imagery in youth sport: promoting the transfer of life skills to other contexts', *Journal of Sport Psychology in Action*, 7(1): 1–10.

Jacobs, J.M. and Wright, P.M. (2018) 'Transfer of life skills in sport-based youth development programs: a conceptual framework bridging learning to application', *Quest*, 70(1): 81–99.

Jacobs, J.M. and Wright, P.M. (2019) 'Thinking about the transfer of life skills: reflections from youth in a community-based sport programme in an underserved urban setting', *International Journal of Sport and Exercise Psychology*, [published online 19 August 2019].

Jacobs, J.M., Wahl-Alexander, Z., and Mack, T. (2019) 'Strategies for gaining access to deliver sport programs with highly vulnerable youth', *Journal of Youth Development*, 14(1): 155–164.

Jacobs, J.M., Lawson, M., Ivy, V.N., and Richards, K.R. (2017) 'Enhancing the transfer of life skills from sport-based youth development programs to school, family, and community settings', *Journal of Amateur Sport*, 3(3): 20–43.

Jenkins, C. and Ellis, T. (2011) 'The highway to hooliganism? An evaluation of the impact of combat sport participation on individual criminality', *International Journal of Police Science and Management*, 13(2): 117–131.

Johansen, P.F. and Green, K. (2019) "Its alpha omega for succeeding and thriving": parents, children and sporting cultivation in Norway', *Sport, Education and Society*, 24(4): 427–440.

Johns, A., Grossman, M., and McDonald, K. (2014) '"More than a game": the impact of sport-based youth mentoring schemes on developing resilience toward violent extremism', *Social Inclusion*, 2(2): 57–70.

Johnson, K. and Maruna, S. (2020) 'Doing justice to desistance narratives', in P. Ugwudike, H. Graham, F. McNeill, P. Raynor, F. Taxman, and C. Trotter (eds), *The Routledge Companion to Rehabilitative Work in Criminal Justice*. Abingdon: Routledge, pp 116–123.

Johnston, J., Harwood, C., and Minniti, A.M. (2013) 'Positive youth development in swimming: clarification and consensus of key psychosocial assets', *Journal of Applied Sport Psychology*, 25(4): 392–411.

Jowett, S. (2017) 'Coaching effectiveness: the coach–athlete relationship at its heart', *Current Opinion in Psychology*, 16: 154–158.

Jugl, I., Bender, D., and Lösel, F. (2021) 'Do sports programs prevent crime and reduce reoffending? A systematic review and meta-analysis on the effectiveness of sports programs', *Journal of Quantitative Criminology*, advance release online.

Jump, D. (2017) 'Why we should think some more: a response to "when you're boxing you don't think so much": pugilism, transitional masculinities and criminal desistance among young Danish gang members', *Journal of Youth Studies*, 20(8): 1093–1107.

Jump, D. (2021) *The Criminology of Boxing, Violence and Desistance*, Bristol: Bristol University Press.

Katz, J. (1988) *Seductions of Crime: Moral and Sensual Attractions in Doing Evil*, New York, NY: Basic Books.

Kelly, L. (2011) '"Social inclusion" through sports-based interventions?', *Critical Social Policy*, 31(1): 126–150.

Kelly, L. (2012a) 'Sport-based interventions and the local governance of youth crime and antisocial behavior', *Journal of Sport and Social Issues*, 37(3): 261–283.

Kelly, L. (2012b) 'Representing and preventing youth crime and disorder: intended and unintended consequences of targeted youth programmes in England', *Youth Justice,* 12(2): 101–117.

Kendellen, K. and Camiré, M. (2015) 'Examining former athletes' developmental experiences in high school sport', *SAGE Open*, 5(4): 1–10.

Kendellen, K. and Camiré, M. (2017) 'Examining the life skill development and transfer experiences of former high school athletes', *International Journal of Sport and Exercise Psychology*, 15(4): 395–408.

Kendellen, K. and Camiré, M. (2019) 'Applying in life the skills learned in sport: a grounded theory', *Psychology of Sport & Exercise*, 40:23–32.

Kendellen, K., Camiré, M., Bean, C., Forneris, T., and Thompson, J. (2017) 'Integrating life skills into Golf Canada's youth programs: insights into a successful research to practice partnership', *Journal of Sport Psychology in Action*, 8(1): 34–46.

Khoury-Kassabri, M. and Schneider, H. (2018) 'The relationship between Israeli youth participation in physical activity programs and antisocial behavior', *Child and Adolescent Social Work Journal*, 35: 357–365.

Klingele, C.M. (2019) 'Measuring change: from rates of recidivism to markers of desistance', *Journal of Criminal Law and Criminology*, 109(4): 769–817.

Knight, C.J. and Newport, R.A. (2017) 'Understanding and working with parents of young athletes', in C.J. Knight, C.G. Harwood, and D. Gould (eds), *Sport Psychology for Young Athletes*, Abingdon: Routledge.

Knight, C.J., Berrow, S.R., and Harwood, C.G. (2017) 'Parenting in sport', *Current Opinion in Psychology*, 16: 93–97.

Kochanek, J., Matthews, A., Wright, E., DiSanti, J., Neff, M., and Erickson, K. (2019) 'Competitive readiness: developmental considerations to promote positive youth development in competitive activities', *Journal of Youth Development*, 14(1): 48–69.

Kreager, D.A. (2007) 'Unnecessary roughness? School sports, peer networks, and male adolescent violence', *American Sociological Review*, 72(5): 705–724.

Lai Chu Fung, A., Ka Hung Lee, T., Fung, A.J.C., and Lee, T.K.H. (2018) 'Effectiveness of Chinese martial arts and philosophy to reduce reactive and proactive aggression in schoolchildren', *Journal of Developmental & Behavioral Pediatrics*, 39(5): 404–414.

Lang, M. and Hartill, M. (2016) *Safeguarding, Child Protection and Abuse in Sport: International Perspectives in Research, Policy and Practice*, London, New York: Routledge.

Larocca, V., Wilson, S., and Cavaliere, A. (2018) 'Examining the association between parent and child sport participation in Canada: a general social survey study', *Canadian Journal of Family and Youth*, 10(1): 171–190.

Laub, J.H. and Sampson, R.J. (2001) 'Understanding desistance from crime', *Crime and Justice*, 28: 1–69.

Laub, J.H. and Sampson, R.J. (2003) *Shared Beginnings, Divergent Lives: Delinquent Boys to Age 70,* Cambridge, MA: Harvard University Press.

Lefebvre, J.S., Evans, M.B., Turnnidge, J., Gainforth, H.L., and Côté, J. (2016) 'Describing and classifying coach development programmes: a synthesis of empirical research and applied practice', *International Journal of Sports Science & Coaching*, 11(6): 887–899.

Lewis, G. and Meek, R. (2012) 'The role of sport in reducing offending among young men in prison: assessing the evidence base', *Forensic Update*, 107: 12–18.

Lim, S.H.R., Koh, K.T., and Chan, M. (2019) '"Two heads are better than one": how supporting staff complement high school sport coaches in promoting positive youth development', *International Sport Coaching Journal*, 6(2): 160–171.

Lipowski, M., Lipowska, M., Jochimek, M., and Krokosz, D. (2016) 'Resiliency as a factor protecting youths from risky behaviour: moderating effects of gender and sport', *European Journal of Sport Science*, 16(2): 246–255.

Lorenz, A. (2018) 'Hierarchy, community, and attachment: integrating at-risk youth into martial arts and combat sports academies', *International Journal of Evidence Based Coaching and Mentoring,* 16(2): 42–54.

Lussier, P., Corrado, R.R., and McCuish, E. (2016) 'A criminal career study of the continuity and discontinuity of sex offending during the adolescence-adulthood transition: a prospective longitudinal study of incarcerated youth', *Justice Quarterly*, 33(7): 1123–1153.

Lussier, P., McCuish, E., and Corrado, R.R. (2015) 'The adolescence–adulthood transition and desistance from crime: examining the underlying structure of desistance', *Journal of Developmental and Life-Course Criminology*, 1(2): 87–117.

Mahoney, J.L. and Stattin, H. (2000) 'Leisure activities and adolescent antisocial behaviour: the role of structure and social context', *Journal of Adolescence*, 23: 113–117.

Martos-García, D., Devís-Devís, J., and Sparkes, A.C. (2009) 'Sport and physical activity in a high security Spanish prison: an ethnographic study of multiple meanings', *Sport, Education and Society*, 14(1): 77–96.

Marttinen, R., Johnston, K., Phillips, S., Fredrick, R.N., and Meza, B. (2019) 'REACH Harlem: young urban boys' experiences in an after-school PA positive youth development program', *Physical Education and Sport Pedagogy*, 24(4): 373–389.

Maruna, S. and Roy, K. (2007) 'Amputation or reconstruction? Notes on the concept of "knifing off" and desistance from crime', *Journal of Contemporary Criminal Justice*, 23(1): 104–124.

Mason, C., Cleland, J., and Aldridge, J. (2017) *Youth Crime Reduction and Sport Pilot Project Evaluation Report*, Loughborough: Loughborough University. Available from: https://allianceofsport.org/insight-hub/youth-crime-reduction-and-sport-pilot-project-evaluation-report/

Matza, D. (1964/1990) *Delinquency and Drift* (1st edn), New York, NY: Routledge.

Mays, D., DePadilla, L., Thompson, N. J., Kushner, H.I., and Windle, M. (2010) 'Sports participation and problem alcohol use: a multi-wave national sample of adolescents', *American Journal of Preventive Medicine*, 38(5): 491–498.

McAra, L., and McVie, S. (2009) 'Youth justice? The impact of system contact on patterns of desistance from offending', in B. Goldson and J. Muncie (eds), *Youth Crime and Juvenile Justice*, London: SAGE Publications.

McDonough, M.H., Ullrich-French, S., Anderson-Butcher, D., Amorose, A.J., and Riley, A. (2013) 'Social responsibility among low-income youth in physical activity-based positive youth development programs: scale development and associations with social relationships', *Journal of Applied Sport Psychology*, 25(4): 431–447.

McHugh, T.-L.F., Coppola, A.M., Holt, N.L., and Andersen, C. (2015) '"Sport is community": an exploration of urban aboriginal peoples' meanings of community within the context of sport', *Psychology of Sport and Exercise*, 18(1): 75–84.

McHugh, T-L.F., Deal, C.J., Blye, C.-J., Dimler, A.J., Halpenny, E.A., Sivak, A. and Holt, N.L. (2019) 'A meta-study of qualitative research examining sport and recreation experiences of indigenous youth', *Qualitative Health Research*, 29(1): 42–54.

McMahon, S. and Belur, J. (2013) *Sports-based Programmes and Reducing Youth Violence and Crime*, London: Project Oracle Children and Youth Evidence Hub.

McNeill, F. (2006) 'A desistance paradigm for offender management', *Criminology and Criminal Justice*, 6(1), 39–62.

McNeill, F. (2021) 'Reducing reoffending and enabling reintegration', in UNAFEI, *Reducing Reoffending: Identifying Risks and Developing Solutions. United Nations Asia and Far East Institute for the Prevention of Crime and the Treatment of Offenders*, Tokyo, Japan. pp 31–44.

McPherson, L., Long, M., Nicholson, M., Cameron, N., Atkins, P., and Morris, M.E. (2017) 'Children's experience of sport in Australia', *Sociology of Sport*, 52(5): 551–569.

Meek, R. (2012) *The Role of Sport in Promoting Desistance from Crime: An Evaluation of the 2nd Chance Project Rugby and Football Academies at Portland Young Offender Institution*, Southampton: University of Southampton.

Meek, R. (2014) *Sport in Prison: Exploring the Role of Physical Activity in Correctional Settings*, Abingdon: Routledge.

Meek, R. (2018) *A Sporting Chance: An Independent Review of Sport in Youth and Adult Prisons*, London: Ministry of Justice.

Meek, R. (2020) 'The use of sport to promote employment, education and desistance from crime: lessons from a review of English and Welsh prisons', in P. Ugwudike, H. Graham, F. McNeill, P. Raynor, F. Taxman, and C. Trotter (eds), *The Routledge Companion to Rehabilitative Work in Criminal Justice*, Abingdon: Routledge, pp 409–418.

Meek, R. and Lewis, G.E. (2014a) 'The impact of a sports initiative for young men in prison: staff and participant perspectives', *Journal of Sport & Social Issues*, 38(2): 95–123.

Meek, R. and Lewis, G.E. (2014b) 'Promoting well-being and desistance through sport and physical activity: the opportunities and barriers experienced by women in English prisons', *Women & Criminal Justice*, 24(2): 151–172.

Meek, R., Champion, N., and Klier, S. (2012) *Fit for Release: How Sport-based Learning Can Help Prisoners Engage in Education, Gain Employment and Desist from Crime*, London: Prisoners' Education Trust.

Miller-Idriss, C. (2020) *Hate in the Homeland: The New Global Far Right*, Princeton, NJ: Princeton University Press.

Mishna, F., Kerr, G., McInroy, L.B., and MacPherson, E. (2019) ' "Student athletes" experiences of bullying in intercollegiate sport', *Journal for the Study of Sports and Athletes in Education*, 13(1): 53–73.

Moffitt, T.E. (1993) 'Adolescence-limited and life-course-persistent antisocial behavior: a developmental taxonomy', *Psychological Review*, 100(4): 674–701.

Morgan, H. (2017) 'Enhancing social mobility within marginalised youth: the accumulation of positive psychological capital through engagement with community sports clubs', *Sport in Society*, 22(11): 1669–1685.

Morgan, H. and Bush, A.J. (2016) 'Sports coach as transformative leader: arresting school disengagement through community sport-based initiatives', *Sport, Education and Society*, 21(5): 759–777.

Morgan, H. and Costas Batlle, I. (2019) 'It's borderline hypocrisy: recruitment practices in youth sport-based interventions', *Journal of Sport for Development*, 7(13): 1–14.

Morgan, H. and Parker, A. (2017) 'Generating recognition, acceptance and social inclusion in marginalised youth populations: the potential of sports-based interventions', *Journal of Youth Studies*, 20(08): 1028–1043.

Morgan, H., Parker, A., and Roberts, W. (2019) 'Community sport programmes and social inclusion: what role for positive psychological capital?', *Sport in Society*, 22(6): 1100–1114.

Morgan, H., Parker, A., Meek, R., and Cryer, J. (2020) 'Participation in sport as a mechanism to transform the lives of young people within the criminal justice system: an academic exploration of a theory of change', *Sport, Education and Society*, 25(8): 917–930.

Morris, L., Sallybanks, J., Willis, K., and Makkai, T. (2004) 'Sport, physical activity and antisocial behaviour in youth', *Youth Studies Australia*, 23(1): 47–52.

Mossman, G.J. and Cronin, L.D. (2019) 'Life skills development and enjoyment in youth soccer: the importance of parental behaviours', *Journal of Sports Sciences*, 37(8): 850–856.

Muirhead, J. and Fortune, C.A. (2016) 'Yoga in prisons: a review of the literature', *Aggression and Violent Behavior*, 28: 57–63.

Mutz, M. and Baur, J. (2009) 'The role of sports for violence prevention: sport club participation and violent behaviour among adolescents', *International Journal of Sport Policy*, 1(3): 305–321.

National Gang Center (2010) 'Best practices to address community gang problems: OJJDP's comprehensive gang model', Washington, DC: Office of Juvenile Justice and Delinquency Prevention. Available from: https://www.ncjrs.gov/pdffiles1/ojjdp/222 799.pdf

Nery, M., Neto, C., Rosado, A., and Smith, P.K. (2019) 'Bullying in youth sport training: a nationwide exploratory and descriptive research in Portugal', *European Journal of Developmental Psychology*, 16(4): 447–463.

Newland, A., Newton, M., Moore, W.G.E., and Legg, W.E. (2019) 'Transformational leadership and positive youth development in basketball', *International Sport Coaching Journal*, 6: 30–41.

Newman, T. K., Kim, Alvarez, M. A. G., and Tucker, A. R. (2018) 'Facilitative coaching: a guide for youth sport leaders', *Leisure/ Loisir*, 42(2): 129–148.

Nichols, G. (1997) 'A consideration of why active participation in sport and leisure might reduce criminal behaviour', *Sport, Education and Society*, 2(2): 181–190.

Nichols, G. (2007) *Sport and Crime Reduction: The Role of Sports in Tackling Youth Crime*, London: Routledge.

Nichols, G. and Crow, I. (2004) 'Measuring the impact of crime reduction interventions involving sports activities for young people', *The Howard Journal*, 43(3): 267–283.

Nite, C. and Nauright, J. (2020) 'Examining institutional work that perpetuates abuse in sport organizations', *Sport Management Review*, 23(1): 117–118.

Noble, J. and Coleman, J. (2016) *Our Theory of Change: Exploring the Role of Sport for Development in the Prevention and Desistance from Crime*. Available from: https://www.sportanddev.org/sites/defa ult/files/downloads/theory_of_change_0.pdf

Nols, Z., Haudenhuyse, R., and Theeboom, M. (2017) 'Urban sport-for-development initiatives and young people in socially vulnerable situations: investigating the "deficit model"', *Social Inclusion*, 5(2): 210–222.

Norman, M. (2017) 'Sport in the underlife of a total institution: social control and resistance in Canadian prisons', *International Review for the Sociology of Sport*, 52(5): 598–614.

Norman, M. and Andrews, G.J. (2019) 'The folding of sport space into carceral space: on the making of prisoners' experiences and lives', *The Canadian Geographer*, 63(3): 453–465.

Osterberg, E.C. (2020) '*We Can't Arrest Our Way Out of This': Police Responses to Gang Violence in British Columbia Lower Mainland*, Doctoral thesis, University of British Columbia, July 2020.

Owusu-Sekyere, F., Rhind, D.J., and Hills, L. (2021) 'Safeguarding culture: towards a new approach to preventing child maltreatment in sport', *Sport Management Review*, 25(2): 300–322.

Parent, S. (2011) 'Disclosure of sexual abuse in sport organizations: a case study', *Journal of Child Sexual Abuse*, 20: 322–337.

Parent, S. and Fortier, K. (2017) 'Prevalence of interpersonal violence against athletes in the sport context', *Current Opinion in Psychology*, 16: 165–169.

Parker, A., Meek, G., and Lewis, G. (2014) 'Sport in a youth prison: male young offenders' experiences of a sporting intervention', *Journal of Youth Studies*, 17(3): 381–396.

Parker, A., Morgan, H., Farooq, S., Moreland, B., and Pitchford, A. (2019) 'Sporting intervention and social change: football, marginalised youth and citizenship development', *Sport, Education and Society*, 24(3): 298–310.

Paylor, I. (2010) 'The scaled approach to youth justice: a risky business', *Criminal Justice Matters*, 81(1): 30–31.

Pennington, C.G. (2017) 'Moral development and sportsmanship in physical education and sport', *Journal of Physical Education, Recreation & Dance*, 88(9): 36–42.

Persson, M., Espedalen, L.E., Stefansen, K., and Strandbu, A. (2019) 'Opting out of youth sports: how can we understand the social processes involved?', *Sport, Education and Society*, 25(2): 1–13.

Petitpas, A.J., Cornelius, A.E., Van Raalte, J.L., and Jones, T. (2005) 'A framework for planning youth sport programs that foster psychosocial development', *The Sport Psychologist*, 19(1): 63–80.

Petrich, D.M. (2020) 'A self-determination theory perspective on human agency, desistance from crime, and correctional rehabilitation', *Journal of Developmental and Life-Course Criminology*, 6(3): 353–379.

Pierce, S., Erickson, K., and Dinu, R. (2019) 'Teacher-coaches' perceptions of life skills transfer from high school sport to the classroom', *Journal of Applied Sport Psychology*, 31(4): 451–473.

Pierce, S., Gould, D.R., and Camiré, M. (2017) 'Definition and model of life skills transfer', *International Review of Sport and Exercise Psychology*, 10(1): 186–211.

Pierce, S., Kendellen, K., Camiré, M., and Gould, D. (2018) 'Strategies for coaching for life skills transfer', *Journal of Sport Psychology in Action*, 9(1): 11–20.

Preston, C. and Fraser-Thomas, J. (2018) 'Problematizing the pursuit of personal development and performance success: an autoethnography of a Canadian elite youth ice hockey coach', *The Sport Psychologist*, 32(2): 102–113.

Preston, C., Allan, V., and Fraser-Thomas, J. (2021) 'Facilitating positive youth development in elite youth hockey: exploring coaches' capabilities, opportunities, and motivations', *Journal of Applied Sport Psychology*, 33(3): 302–320.

Psychou, D., Kokaridas, D., Koularis, N., Theodorakis, Y., and Krommidas, C. (2019) 'The effect of exercise on improving quality of life and self-esteem of inmates in Greek prisons', *Journal of Human Sport and Exercise*, 14(2): 374–384.

Public Safety Canada (2017) *Research Highlights: Sport-Based Crime Prevention Programs*, Ottawa: PSC. Available from: https://www.publicsafety.gc.ca/cnt/rsrcs/pblctns/2017-h03-cp/2017-h03-cp-en.pdf

Quarmby, T. (2014) 'Sport and physical activity in the lives of looked-after children: a "hidden group" in research, policy and practice', *Sport, Education and Society*, 19(7): 944–958.

Quilico, E.L., Harvey, W.J., Caron, J.G., and Bloom, G.A. (2021) 'Interpretative phenomenological analysis of community exercise experiences after severe traumatic brain injury', *Qualitative Research in Sport, Exercise and Health*, 13(5): 800–815.

RAN Centre of Excellence (2019) *The Role of Sports and Leisure Activities in Preventing and Countering Violent Extremism*. Available from: https://ec.europa.eu/home-affairs/sites/homeaffairs/files/what-we-do/networks/radicalisation_awareness_network/about-ran/ran-yf-and-c/docs/ran_yfc_sports_and_leisure_06-07_03_2019_en.pdf

Reverdito, R.S., Galatti, L.R., Carvalho, H.M., Scaglia, A.J., Cote, J., Goncalves, C.E., and Paes, R.R. (2017) 'Developmental benefits of extracurricular sports participation among Brazilian youth', *Perceptual and Motor Skills*, 125(5): 946–960.

Rich, K., Bean, C., and Apramian, Z. (2014) 'Boozing, brawling, and community building: sport-facilitated community development in a rural Ontario community', *Leisure/Loisir*, 38(1): 73–91.

Richardson, C., Cameron, P.A., and Berlouis, K.M. (2017) 'The role of sport in deradicalisation and crime diversion', *Journal for Deradicalization*, 13: 29–48.

Riciputi, S., McDonough, M.H., Snyder, F.J., and McDavid, M.L. (2020) 'Staff support promotes engagement in a physical activity-based positive youth development program for youth from low-income families', *Sport, Exercise, and Performance Psychology*, 9(1): 45–57.

Riley, A., Anderson-Butcher, D., Logan, J., Newman, T.J., and Davis, J. (2017) 'Staff practices and social skill outcomes in a sport-based youth program', *Journal of Applied Sport Psychology*, 29(1): 59–74.

Roberts, V., Sojo, V., and Grant, F. (2020) 'Organisational factors and non-accidental violence in sport: a systematic review', *Sport Management Review*, 23(1): 8–27.

Roe, D., Hugo, M., and Larsson, H. (2019) ' "Rings on the water": examining the pedagogical approach at a football program for detained youth in Sweden', *Sport in Society*, 22(6): 919–934.

Ronkainen, N.J., Aggerholm, K., Ryba, T.V., and Allen-Collinson, J. (2021) 'Learning in sport: from life skills to existential learning', *Sport, Education and Society*, 26(2): 214–227.

Ropeik, D. (2010) *How Risky Is It Really: Why Our Fears Don't Always Match the Facts*, New York: McGraw Hill.

Roth, J.L. and Brooks-Gunn, J. (2016) 'Evaluating youth development programs: progress and promise', *Applied Developmental Science*, 20(3): 188–202.

Ruppé, W., Sirosta, O., Durand, C., and Dermit, N. (2020) 'Measuring the violence and incivility of players in professional sport and the disciplinary bodies' management: statistical analysis of French professional football', *Sports in Society*, 23(6): 981–1003.

Rutten, E.A., Stams, G.J.J.M., Biesta, G.J.J., Schuengel, C., Dirks, E., and Hoeksma, J.B. (2007) 'The contribution of organized youth sport to antisocial and prosocial behavior in adolescent athletes', *Journal of Youth and Adolescence*, 36(3): 255–264.

Samuel, K.J.T. (2018) *Desk Review on Sport as a Tool for the Prevention of Violent Extremism*, Vienna: United Nations Office on Drugs and Crime.

Sandford, R.A., Armour, K., and Duncombe, R. (2007) 'Physical activity and personal/social development for disaffected youth in the UK: in search of evidence', in N. Holt (ed), *Positive Youth Development through Sport*, London: Routledge, pp 97–109.

Sandford, R.A., Armour, K.M., and Warmington, P. (2006) 'Re-engaging disaffected youth through physical activity programmes', *British Educational Research Journal*, 32(2): 251–71.

Sandford, R.A., Duncombe, R., and Armour, K.M. (2008) 'The role of physical activity/sport in tackling youth disaffection and anti-social behaviour', *Educational Review*, 60(4): 419–435.

Santos, F., Strachan, L., and Pereira, P. (2019) 'How to promote positive youth development in physical education? The experiences of a physical educator and students through the delivery of Project SCORE', *The Physical Educator*, 76: 1002–1025.

Scheithauer, H., Leppin, N., and Hess, M. (2020) 'Preventive interventions for children in organized team sport tackling aggression: results from the pilot evaluation of "Fairplayer. Sport"', *New Directions for Child and Adolescent Development*, 2020(173): 49–63.

Schwenzer, V., Behn, S., Cravo, S., Martinez, R., Moreno, J, and Rico, R. (2007) *Sports Activities for the Prevention of Youth Violence and Crime*, Berlin: AGIS.

Sempé, G. (2018) *Sport and Prisons in Europe*, Strasbourg: Council of Europe Publishing.

Shannon, C.S. (2013) 'Bulling in recreation and sport settings: exploring risk factors, prevention efforts, and intervention strategies', *Journal of Park and Recreation Administration*, 31(1): 15–33.

Sheppard, A.C. and Mahoney, J.L. (2012) 'Time spent in sports and adolescent problem behaviors: a longitudinal analysis of directions of association', *Journal of Youth Development*, 7(3): 87–101.

Sheppard-Marks, L., Shipway, R., and Brown, L. (2020) 'Life at the edge: exploring male athlete criminality', *Sport in Society*, 23(6): 1042–1062.

Sherry, E. and Strybosch, V. (2012) 'A kick in the right direction: longitudinal outcomes of the Australian Community Street Soccer program', *Soccer & Society*, 13(4): 495–509.

Skinner, J. and Zakus, D.H. (2008) 'Development through sport: building social capital in disadvantaged communities', *Sport Management Review*, 11: 253–275.

Smith, C., Roy, L., Peck, S., and Macleod, C. (2017) *Evaluation of Program Quality and Social and Emotional Learning in American Youth Circus Organization Social Circus Programs*, Ypsilnanti, MI: The David P. Weikart Center for Youth Program Quality.

Søgaard, T.F., Kolind, T., Thylstrup, B., and Deuchar, R. (2016) 'Desistance and the micro-narrative construction of reformed masculinities in a Danish rehabilitation centre', *Criminology & Criminal Justice* 16 (1): 99–118.

Spaaij, R. (2012) 'Building social and cultural capital among young people in disadvantaged communities: lessons from a Brazilian sport-based intervention program', *Sport, Education and Society*, 17(1): 77–95.

Spruit, A., Vugt, E., Put, C., Stouwe, T., and Stams, G.J. (2016) 'Sports participation and juvenile delinquency: a meta-analytic review', *Journal of Youth and Adolescence*, 45(4): 655–671.

Spruit, A., Hoffenaar, P., van der Put, C., van Vugt, E. and Stams, G.J. (2018a) 'The effect of a sport-based intervention to prevent juvenile delinquency in at-risk adolescents', *Children and Youth Services Review*, 94(4): 689–698.

Spruit, A., van der Put, C., van Vugt, E., and Stams, G.J. (2018b) 'Predictors of intervention success in a sport-based program for adolescents at risk of juvenile delinquency', *International Journal of Offender Therapy and Comparative Criminology*, 62(6): 1535–1555.

Stafford, A., Alexander, K., and Fry, D. (2013) 'Playing through pain: children and young people's experiences of physical aggression and violence in sport', *Child Abuse Review*, 22(4): 287–299.

Stansfield, R. (2017) 'Teen development in sports and risky behaviour: a cross-national and gender analysis', *The British Journal of Criminology*, 57(1): 172–193.

Steinfeldt, J.A., Foltz, B.D., Mungro, J., Speight, Q.L., Wong, Y.J., and Blumberg, J. (2011) 'Masculinity socialization in sports: influence of college football coaches', *Psychology of Men & Masculinity*, 12(3): 247–259.

Stodolksa, M., Shinew, K.J., and Acevedo, J.C. (2013) '"I was born in the hood": fear of crime, outdoor recreation and physical activity among Mexican-American urban adolescents', *Leisure Sciences*, 35: 1–15.

Strachan, L., McHugh, T.L., and Mason, C. (2018) 'Understanding positive youth development in sport through the voices of indigenous youth', *Journal of Sport and Exercise Psychology*, 40: 293–302.

Sullivan, T.N., Farrell, A.D., Bettencourt, A.F., and Helms, S.W. (2008) 'Core competencies and the prevention of youth violence', *New Directions for Child and Adolescent Development*, 122: 33–46.

Super, S., Verkooijen, K., and Koelen, M. (2018) 'The role of community sports coaches in creating optimal social conditions for life skill development and transferability: a salutogenic perspective', *Sport, Education and Society*, 23(2): 173–185.

Super, S., Wentink, C.Q., Verkooijen, K.T., and Koelen, M.A. (2017) 'Exploring the sports experiences of socially vulnerable youth', *Social Inclusion*, 5(2): 1–12.

Super, S., Wentink, C.Q., Verkooijen, K.T., and Koelen, M.A. (2019) 'How young adults reflect on the role of sport in their socially vulnerable childhood', *Qualitative Research in Sport, Exercise and Health*, 11(1): 20–34.

Sutcliffe, J. T., McLaren, C. D., Benson, A. J., Martin, L. J., Arnocky, S., Shields, C., et al. (2020) 'Parents' moral intentions towards antisocial parent behaviour: an identity approach in youth sport', *Psychology of Sport and Exercise*, 49: Article 101699 [published online].

Taylor, M.J., Nanney, J.T., Welch, D.S., and Wamser-Nanney, R.A. (2016) *The impact of sports participation on female gang involvement and delinquency, Journal of Sport Behavior*, 39(3): 317–343.

Terry-McElrath, Y.M., O'Malley, P.M., and Johnston, L.D. (2011) 'Exercise and substance use among American youth, 1991–2009', *American Journal of Preventive Medicine*, 40(5): 530–540.

Thailand Institute of Justice (2019) *A New Chapter of Youth Crime Prevention and Criminal Justice through Sports*. Available from: https://www.tijthailand.org/highlight/detail/232

Tolan, P., Henry, D., Schoeny, M., Bass, A., Lovergrove, P., and Nichols, E. (2013) *Mentoring Interventions to Affect Juvenile Delinquency and Associated Problems: A Systematic Review*, Campbell Systematic Reviews 2013, 10.

Tolan, P., Ross, K., Arkin, N., Godine, N., and Clark, E. (2016) 'Toward an integrated approach to positive development: implications for interventions', *Applied Developmental Science*, 20(3): 214–36.

Trottier, C. and Robitaille, S. (2014) 'Fostering life skills development in high school and community sport: a comparative analysis of the coach's role', *The Sport Psychologist*, 28(1): 10–21.

Turgeon, S., Kendellen, K., Kramers, S., Rathwell, S., and Camiré, M. (2019) 'Making high school sport impactful', *Kinesiology Review,* 8: 188–194.

Turnnidge, J. and Côté, J. (2017) 'Transformational coaching workshop: applying a personal approach to coach development programs', *International Sport Coaching Journal*, 4(3): 314–325.

Turnnidge, J. and Côté, J. (2018) 'Applying transformational leadership theory to coaching research in youth sport: a systematic literature review', *International Journal of Sport and Exercise Psychology*, 16(3): 327–342.

Turnnidge, J., Côté, J., and Hancock, D.J. (2014) 'Positive youth development from sport to life: explicit or implicit transfer?', *Quest*, 66(2): 203–217.

United Nations (2015) *Nelson Mandela Rules*, General Assembly Resolution 70/175, annex, adopted on 17 December 2015.

United Nations (2017) 'Sport as a Means to Promote Education, Health, Development and Peace', A/RES/71/160, 2017. Available from: https://documents-dds-ny.un.org/doc/UNDOC/GEN/N16/449/81/PDF/N1644981.pdf?OpenElement

United Nations (2020) *Outcome of the Expert Group Meeting on Integrating Sport into Youth Crime Prevention and Criminal Justice Strategies*, Report of the Secretary General, April 2020, E/CN.15/2020/14. Available from: V2001511.pdf (un.org)

United Nations Office on Drugs and Crime (2017) *Line Up Live Up Trainer Manual: Life Skills Training Through Sport to Prevent Crime, Reduce Violence and Drug Use*, Vienna: United Nations. Available from: https://www.unodc.org/documents/dohadeclaration/Sports/LULU/Manual/LULU_Manual_EN.pdf

United Nations Office on Drugs and Crime (2020a) *Youth Crime Prevention Through Sport: Insights from the UNODC 'Line Up Live Up' Pilot Programme*, Vienna: UNODC.

United Nations Office on Drugs and Crime (2020b) *Preventing Violent Extremism Through Sport: Technical Guide*, Vienna: United Nations.

Vaccaro, C.A., Schrock, D.P., and McCabe, J.M. (2011) 'Managing emotional manhood in the cage: masculinity and mixed martial arts', *Social Psychology Quarterly*, 74(4): 414–437.

Vandermeerschen, H., Vos, S., and Scheerder, J. (2013) 'Who's joining the club? Participation of socially vulnerable children and adolescents in club organised sports', *Sport, Education and Society*, 8: 941–958.

Veliz, P., Eckner, J.T., Zdroik, J., and Schulenberg, J.E. (2019) 'Lifetime prevalence of self-reported concussion among adolescents involved in competitive sports: a national U.S. study', *Journal of Adolescent Health*, 64(2): 272–275.

Veliz, P., Ryan, J., and Eckner, J.T. (2021) 'Head, neck, and traumatic brain injury among children involved in sports: results from the adolescent brain cognitive development study', *Journal of Adolescent Health*, 68(4): 414–418.

Vella, S.A., Oades, L.G., and Crowe, T.P. (2011) 'The role of the coach in facilitating positive youth development: moving from theory to practice', *Journal of Applied Sport Psychology*, 23(1): 33–48.

Vella, S.A., Oades, L.G., and Crowe, T.P. (2013) 'The relationship between coach leadership, the coach–athlete relationship, team success, and the positive developmental experiences of adolescent soccer players', *Physical Education and Sport Pedagogy*, 18(5): 549–561.

Vertommen, T., Schipper-van Veldhoven, N., Wouters, K., Kampen, J.K., Brackenridge, C.H., Rhind, D.J.A., Neels, K., and Van Den Eedea, F. (2016) 'Interpersonal violence against children in sport in the Netherlands and Belgium', *Child Abuse & Neglect*, 51: 223–236.

Vertommen, T., Kampen, J., Schipper-van Veldhoven, N., Uzieblo, K., and Van Den Eede, F. (2018) 'Severe interpersonal violence against children in sport: associated mental health problems and quality of life in adulthood', *Child Abuse & Neglect*, 76: 459–468.

Vertonghen, J. and Theeboom, M. (2010) 'The social-psychological outcomes of martial arts practise among youth: a review', *Journal of Sports Science and Medicine*, 9(4): 528–537.

Vierimaa, M., Erickson, K., Côté, J., and Gilbert, W. (2012) 'Positive youth development: a measurement framework for sport', *International Journal of Sport Science and Coaching*, 7(3): 601–614.

Vierimaa, M., Turnnidge, J., Bruner, M., and Côté, J. (2017) 'Just for the fun of it: coaches' perceptions of an exemplary community youth sport program', *Physical Education and Sport Pedagogy*, 22(6): 603–617.

Villeneuve, M.P., F-Dufour, I., and Farrall, S. (2021) 'Assisted desistance in formal settings: a scoping review', *Howard Journal of Criminal Justice*, 60(1): 75–100.

Waid, J. and Uhrich, M (2020) 'A scoping review of the theory and practice of positive youth development', *British Journal of Social Work*, 50(1): 5–24.

Waller, I. (2014) *Smarter Crime Control: A Guide to Safer Future for Citizens, Communities, and Politicians*, Lanham, MD: Rowman & Littlefield.

Weaver, B. (2017) *Offending and Desistance: The Importance of Social Relations*, London: Routledge.

Weiss, M.R. and Wiese-Bjornstal, D.M. (2009) 'Promoting positive youth development through physical activity', *President's Council on Physical Fitness and Sports Research Digest*, 19: 1–8.

Weiss, M.R., Stuntz, C.P., Bhalla, J.A., Bolter, N.D., and Price, M.S. (2013) '"More than a game": impact of the First Tee life skills programme on positive youth development: project introduction and year 1 findings', *Qualitative Research in Sport, Exercise and Health*, 85(3): 214–244.

Weiss, M.R., Bolter, N.D., and Kipp, L.E. (2014) 'Assessing impact of physical activity-based youth development programs: validation of the Life Skills Transfer Survey (LSTS)', *Research Quarterly for Exercise and Sport*, 85(3): 263–278.

Weiss, M.R., Bolter, N.D., and Kipp, L.E. (2016) 'Evaluation of the first tee in promoting positive youth development: group comparisons and longitudinal trends', *Research Quarterly for Exercise and Sport*, 87(3): 271–283.

Whatman, S.L. and Main, L. (2018) 'Re-engaging "youth at risk" of disengaging from schooling through rugby league club partnership: unpacking the pedagogic practices of the Titans Learning Centre', *Sport, Education and Society*, 23(4): 339–353.

Whitley, M.A., Massey, W.V., and Wilkinson, M. (2018) 'A systems theory of development through sport for traumatized and disadvantaged youth', *Psychology of Sport & Exercise*, 38: 116–125.

Williams, D., Collingwood, L., Coles, J., and Schmeer, S. (2015) 'Evaluating a rugby sport intervention programme for young offenders', *Journal of Criminal Psychology*, 5(1): 51–64.

Williams, H. (2012) *Repairing Shattered Lives: Brain Injury and Its Implications for Criminal Justice*, London: Barrow Cadbury Trust.

Wilson, W.J. (1996) *When Work Disappears*, New York, NY: Knopf.

Wimberly, A.S. and Engstrom, M. (2018) 'Stress, substance use, and yoga in the context of community re-entry following incarceration', *Journal of Correctional Health Care*, 24(1): 96–203.

Woods, D., Breslin, G., and Hassan, D. (2017a) 'A systematic review of the impact of sport-based interventions on the psychological well-being of people in prison', *Mental Health and Physical Activity*, 12: 50–61.

Woods, D., Breslin, G., and Hassan, D. (2017b) 'Positive collateral damage or purposeful design: how sport-based interventions impact the psychological well-being of people in prison', *Mental Health and Physical Activity*, 13: 152–162.

World Health Organization (1999) *Partners in Life Skills Education*. Available from: https://phkh.nhsrc.pk/sites/default/files/2020-01/A4_52RF_Patterns%20in%20life%20skill%20education.pdf

Wright, P.M., Jacobs, J.M., Howell, S.M., and McLoughlin, G.M. (2020) 'Implementation and perceived benefits of an after-school soccer program designed to promote social and emotional learning: a multiple case study', *Journal of Amateur Sport*, 6(1): 125–145.

Zeldin, S. (2004) 'Preventing youth violence through the promotion of community engagement and membership', *Journal of Community Psychology*, 32(5): 623–641.

Index

References to figures appear in *italic* type. References to endnotes show both the page number and the note number (131n2).